OUT OF DARKNESS...
INTO THE LIGHT

OUT OF DARKNESS...
INTO THE LIGHT

LAURIE WALLACE

AMBASSADOR HOUSE
WESTMINSTER, COLORADO

Out of Darkness...Into the Light. Copyright © 1995 by Laurie Wallace. Published by Ambassador House, P.O. Box 1153, Westminster, Colorado 80030, phone: (303) 369-4056 *and* Laurie Laurie Wallace Email Address 77030 victory1@www.isp.com

All rights reserved. No part of this publication may be reproduced, stored in a retrieval system, or transmitted in any form by means electronic, mechanical, photocopy, recording, or otherwise without the prior permission of the publisher, except as provided by USA copyright law.

Cover design: Brandon Kirk

Revised Edition 1998

Scripture quotations are from the King James Version of the Holy Bible.

Printed in the United States of America.

ISBN: 0-9663533-1-5

If unavailable in local bookstores, additional copies of this publication may be purchased by writing or calling the publisher at the above address.

This book is dedicated:

To my Lord, Jesus Christ, to Whom I owe my life, for shedding His precious blood and dying for me. Because He lives, I can face tomorrow!

—And—

To my sweet and loving mother

—for all the things you taught me as a child growing up in God's Word;

—for all the times you gave me little cards and told me how very much you loved me and how very much God loved me too, how He was my dearest friend;

—for all the times you prayed for me during my youth when I was rebellious towards you and Dad;

—for trusting me into God's hands and believing He would deliver me out of any situation I may come to face.

Thank you for your strength and faith. Thank you for being grounded in the Word, for always telling me God had a special plan for my life.

Without your love, support, and beautiful spirit, I would not be here today! My loving thanks to you, Mother. I love you very much!

Acknowledgments

Thanks to my father, brother, and baby sister for your support throughout this experience, and for your continued telephone calls to me before I went into the hospital and during the time I was there. I could not have made it without my loving family.

Thanks to my loving grandparents, Big Mama and Big Daddy, for always believing in me, for all the times you gave me comfort as a child when I was hurting, and for all the love you poured out to me throughout my life.

Thanks to my two friends who were with me in Houston during the time I was sick and in the hospital. The two of you helped me through the most frightening experience of my life. I truly appreciate your support and friendship. May God bless you a hundred-fold.

Thanks to Aunt Lina for the many times you would pray with me over the telephone after I left the hospital while I was recovering. God could not have blessed me with a better prayer partner. Thank you so much.

My special thanks to Dr. Charles Kraft of Fuller Theological Seminary in California. I appreciate your tips on writing and how to present my personal story.

Thanks to the many friends I've made in church who have enriched my life so and have been there for support throughout this experience. Thanks for your words of encouragement in fighting this battle of spiritual warfare and for standing with me.

CONTENTS

Preface		xv
Introduction		xix
Chapter 1	My Childhood Years	21
Chapter 2	Becoming a Woman	41
Chapter 3	Saying Good-Bye	55
Chapter 4	How I Was Enticed	63
Chapter 5	Dabbling with the Occult	73
Chapter 6	Afflicted with Sickness	91
Chapter 7	Tricked by an Angel of Light	97
Chapter 8	Proving My Faith in Jesus	119
Chapter 9	In Closing	153
Chapter 10	Looking Forward	161

But ye are a chosen generation, a royal priesthood, an holy nation, a peculiar people; that ye should shew forth the praises of Him who hath called you out of darkness into His marvelous light.

1 Peter 2:9

PREFACE

This is the story of someone who could have been your sister, daughter, or granddaughter—someone who grew up as a typical young American woman with all the bright hopes and expectations to which any young lady has a right. But she got caught in a trap, a trap laid carefully by an enemy she didn't know was there and certainly didn't know how to counter.

Our society is being used by this enemy to produce people like Laurie once was, people who are feeling discouraged and powerless, looking for meaning anywhere they can find it. Many Americans no longer believe in the invisible dark angels who populate Satan's kingdom and, therefore, we fall easy prey to them as they quietly take advantage of our attitudes and the structures of the society around us. We are morally and spiritually adrift, disillusioned with the satisfactions provided by the basic institutions of our society—science, government, business, education, our legal system, even church.

We are, therefore, sitting ducks for the enemy's schemes as he uses those around us to promise us the things we think we want: power, position, and whatever else will feed our self-interest.

OUT OF DARKNESS...INTO THE LIGHT

As a member of this kind of society, Laurie Wallace was set up for just such promises. She was not a bad person. She was only looking for what she had been promised. And she became a victim produced by a society which offers few answers that work and even fewer that satisfy. She knew Christ, but her Christianity had become dull and lifeless and she had not been properly warned by her church about the enemy who, though sometimes he "roams around like a roaring lion" (I Peter 5:8), can also disguise himself as an "angel of light" (II Corinthians 11:14).

So Laurie, like many of her generation, wandered into dangerous places, looking for meaning, listening to promises, seeking enough power to attain goals she had been led to expect she deserved. And she, like too many of our young people, soon became caught in a web she could not see, serving a master she didn't even know was there.

Although she—part consciously, mostly unconsciously—chose against God, He never gave up on her. She had not completely lost her ability to discern right from wrong, so in her moment of triumph, just when by using the enemy's power she was accomplishing what she most wanted, she allowed herself to hear God's voice. But the enemy's evil web was strong and she was well tangled up in it. By drawing on the power of Satan's demons to get what she wanted, Laurie had given them an incredible amount of power over her, so it was literally a life-and-death struggle from that point on to work with God to extricate herself from their clutches. But she and God won.

Laurie's story has a happy ending. It points, however, to a very sad situation. The enemy who entrapped Laurie is still on the loose and our society is still producing unwitting victims by the thousands. Yet our churches, though endued with the power of Christ to defeat the Evil One, are still ignorant both of the enemy's devices and of how to rescue those still caught in his web.

May this volume be used by God to wake us up both to the problem and to the solution. Our sisters, daughters, brothers, and sons are too valuable, both to God and to us, for them to have to go through what Laurie went through.

Dr. Charles H. Kraft
Fuller Theological Seminary

INTRODUCTION

I could not go on with my life without sharing the most horrifying experience that happened to me when I was caught up with the fascination and the mysticism of the New Age. We live in a world today filled with the curiosity of how to be master of our own lives and how to unleash the powers of the subconscious mind.

You can walk into almost any bookstore and find aisles overflowing with books about the New Age we are living in, a New Age that is no longer the Church Age. We rarely hear, "Thy will be done" but rather, "My will be done."

With today's rising fascination with powers of the occult and the New Age Movement, I know how crucial it is that I speak out now before it becomes too late for others. It took me a full year to become strong enough to deal with the opposition, the forces of evil.

What happened to me on October 22, 1993, was the most horrifying and traumatic experience of my life. Whenever I wonder why I am still alive, I know it is truly by an act of my faith and God's grace. I am alive because God has given me a "second chance" and, because of that, I must share this experience with others. I pray God uses this book to touch the lives of those crying out for His love, His mercy, and His forgiveness.

My intent is to open your eyes so you may turn from darkness to light, and from the power of Satan unto God!

This book was written for you, my reader.

Chapter One

MY CHILDHOOD YEARS

In the early years of my childhood, I had, what I considered to be a happy, normal life. I hardly expected the happiness I once knew would turn into such tragedy. The disaster I encountered is more horrid than one can imagine. An evil force peacefully led me straight into the abyss of hell. I was never warned of the danger that lurks in darkness and I never knew there was an enemy hard at work behind the scenes—until one night when I met him face to face! First, allow me to give you some background.

I grew up in a small town in Alabama. I regularly attended a local Baptist church with my mother, a younger brother, and my baby sister. I felt, since I was two years older than my brother, David (not his real name), and eight years older than my little sister, Rebecca (not her real name), I was the one to set an example for the other two. Being the first child, I also felt I was the instigator of all mistakes made.

At the early age of eight, I accepted Jesus Christ as my personal Saviour. I was so happy when I was baptized in our local church. I remember it as though it were yesterday. I stood when the pastor gave the invitation and said, "All of those who would like to accept Christ as your personal Saviour, please quietly get up out of your seats and come down to the front of the church and kneel at the altar." I felt a tingly sensation all over my body for the very first time. It is what I now call "holy bumps," the feeling that comes when you know a true message from God is being revealed to your spirit.

I knew at this time that Christ died for me, and I invited him into my heart. I walked down the aisle, knelt, and prayed. Moments later, my mother came and joined me. At the close of the service, Reverend Fields presented to the congregation of the church those who had accepted Christ that Sunday. When he got to me, he announced my name and said, "This baby—this little child—has come to know Jesus; thank you, Lord, for the little children of this church, for a child shall lead the way." I went to Reverend Fields' study afterwards and talked with him about Jesus. Reverend Fields was such a sweet and godly man.

Much of my youth was spent being very active in the church. I belonged to Girls Auxiliary, sang in the youth choir, and loved to go to summer camp at Camp Winetaska.

Reverend Fields baptized me at First Baptist Church. I was so small and frightened that I thought I would surely drown in that pool of water. Reverend Fields stood about 5'10", was in his fifties, and had gray hair and round, rosy cheeks.

I loved going to church and seeing Brother Fields. He was the type of man who adored the little children of our church. I fondly remember him standing at the door of the church after the service on Sundays, greeting and shaking hands with all the members and handing out candy to all of us children as we passed him by. When I would go to church on Wednesday nights, I would always find my way into his office, hoping to see him and, of course, get some candy.

His office was unlike any other pastoral study I have ever seen. The walls were richly decorated in a deep purple. He loved the color purple because he said it reminded him of his King, Jesus.

Brother Fields especially loved to visit the zoo. Many times my mother would take me to the zoo in the summertime, and often we would see him there. Even the monkeys remembered him as he would often give them candy also.

For many years, the only children in my family were my brother and me. I was a typical older sister and, of course, overbearing. I must have used creative visualization at an early age because I remember, well before my sister was born, telling all of my friends' mothers that my mommy was going to have a baby. Some of them called her on the phone and asked, "Ruth (not her real name), are you pregnant?"

She would reply, "Why heavens no! Where on earth did you get such an idea?"

Mother would ask, "Laurie, why on earth do you keep saying these things?" I would reply, "Mommy, I want you to have a baby." How I must have tried my mother's patience even at such an early age.

My sister was born when I was eight. It was a miracle that she was even born. My mother, at seven months pregnant, weighed only 120 pounds. My mother's body tried to reject the pregnancy. The doctor told my family that, if my mother carried the baby to full term, there was a chance something could be wrong with the baby.

On February 21, 1973, our precious baby girl, Rebecca, was born. She was so beautiful and healthy, so perfect and full of life. Reverend Fields declared she was indeed a "miracle baby," and to us she most certainly was.

My mother was raised in a Baptist church in Alabama and was gifted with a very beautiful voice. She sang in the church choir and professionally with a ladies' ensemble called "New Creation." We traveled to different churches in Alabama where her group would sing. I would sit in church on Sundays when she sang a solo, and listening to her voice would delight my heart. I would think to myself, "That's my mom!"

My mother's love and beautiful spirit had a great impact upon my life. She always took a special interest in each of her children. I fondly reflect back to the times she would give me little cards to tell me how much she loved me. When I was eighteen years old in December of 1982, she gave me a Bible for Christmas. These are the words she lovingly wrote to me:

Dearest Laurie:

You are a woman now, and I've tried to mold you and guide you into all truth and knowledge. To me, you will always be my little girl, but I know that I have to acknowledge the fact that you are a woman.

My prayer for you, is that you follow God's path and plan for your life, because you will be happy and victorious in everything. You have so many good qualities that the Lord would like to make use of. Always listen to His Holy Spirit, because He is your dearest true friend.

Read and keep these Words of God's Book in your Heart Always.

"*In all thy ways acknowledge Him, and He will direct thy paths.*"
Proverbs 3:6

*Lovingly,
Mother*

These words taken from the front of my Bible were one of the many ways my mother showed her love for me. She did little things that meant so much to me as a child growing up. God could not have made a better choice in mothers than the one He chose for me. As a small child, a teenager, and an adult, my mother has always been there for me.

Once, when I was a small child, my mother would not let me have my way about something, so I decided to run away from home. I packed my little suitcase with my toothbrush and an extra change of panties and off I went. I said, "Mommy, I am running away."

She replied, "Okay, Laurie, but where will you sleep?" I said, "I will sleep somewhere."

"What will you eat?" she asked.

"I will find something to eat," I responded.

She said, "All right, Mommy loves you and I am going to miss you very much."

I took a step off the front porch and was halfway down the driveway, walking as fast as my little feet would carry me, when all of a sudden I turned around and looked back. There she stood on the front porch with tears in her eyes looking at me. I burst into tears, went running back up the driveway, jumped into her arms, and said, "Mommy, I love you. I could never leave you." Needless to say, that was the end of that.

My father, a well-built, handsome man, grew up in Alabama as well. He did not have roots in the church as did my mother, and therefore, he never really had much interest in going to church with our family. Before my birth, my father was in the Marines. Years later, he took a position in public service that carried a lot of responsibility. Time for his family was very limited. Throughout much of my early childhood and my youth, my father was absent.

By the time I reached the age of twelve, my parents started having marital problems and for many years were married in name only. My father began to drink heavily and had affairs with different women. As a child, this caused me a great deal of embarrassment in our community since my father was a well-known public figure.

When my father drank, he became violent. I was so ashamed to bring friends home with me in fear of some explosive behavior. My father was very abusive when he drank. Many times he would come home drunk during the middle of the night, and I would hear my mother and him in their bedroom fighting. I was so protective of my mother that I would go into their bedroom and try to break up their fighting, only to get hit myself.

Many times my father's eruptions would affect me so badly I was unable to attend school the following day. At this time in my life, I hated him for all the pain he caused my family. Many times I begged my mother to divorce him, but she could not for fear of how she would raise three children alone. She kept telling me God was going to change him.

I cannot even count the times I would walk into her bedroom and find her crying on her hands and knees,

MY CHILDHOOD YEARS

holding her Bible at her side, praying and asking God to change him.

I spent many tearful and emotional years in this sort of environment before my parents divorced. The longer I stayed in it, the more I rebelled against God. Even though my parents did finally divorce, the mental and spiritual damage to me had already been done. Only now can I see the foothold that demons had early in my life as I had been inhabited by a demon spirit of rebellion. Demons came into me during my youth through my damaged emotions. Spoken curses were inflicted upon me through the verbal abuse of my father.

Little did I perceive that I had become the victim of malicious works taking place in an unseen realm. A work so detestable it has attempted to annihilate the family values of this once great nation.

I no longer enjoyed attending church in my teen years, as I did when I was a young child. In fact, I refused to go to church on Sunday. My mother would try to make me go, but I would always have an excuse and would cause her to be late every Sunday; I gave her no choice but to go without me.

I had developed such a resentment about church, and I guess, even toward God. I felt that, if there really was a God, then why did He not change my father? After all, mother always told me, "God was going to change him." This was the biggest mistake I could have ever made in life—allowing myself to get mad at God.

The verbal and physical abuse from my father was more than I could bear. My father continuously spoke curses over my life. "Death and life are in the power of the tongue," *Proverbs 18:21*. Spoken words have power to either bless or curse. When dealing with word curses we must consider (1) Evil words that others have spoken against us. (2) Evil words that we have spoken against others. (3) Evil words that we have spoken against ourselves.

Evil words can produce curses, not only when they are spoken maliciously, but also when spoken carelessly. This is why it is so very important that we learn to discipline our tongues on the one hand, and, on the other hand, break the power of words that speak ill of us.

When we speak evil of others, we curse them. The word of God commands that we "bless, and curse not" *Romans 12:14*. Therefore, cursing others brings a curse upon oneself. Disobedience to God's command not to curse others will bring a curse *(See: Deuteronomy 27:26)*. Jesus taught:

> *But I say unto you, Love your enemies, bless them that curse you, do good to them that hate you, and pray for them which despitefully use you, and persecute you.*
>
> *Matthew 5:44*

It is sobering, to say the least, that each of us will give an account of our words on the day of judgment.

> *But I say unto you, That every idle word that men shall speak, they shall give account thereof in the day of judgment.*
>
> *Matthew 12:36*

Too often cursing of others takes place within families. Parents curse their children with such words as, "You're not good; you'll never amount to anything;

you're stupid," or similar references. As in my case with the verbal abuse and spoken words over my life from my father. Such children often grow up to be failures who never succeed in life, because of the negative pronouncements made over them by their parents. They are cursed children. Demons are the enforcers of their curse. Children curse parents when they dishonor and express disrespect by disdain, impudence, sassiness and back talk.

Husbands and wives curse one another when they belittle, criticize and condemn one another instead of showing mutual love and respect. Husbands and wives should realize they have become "one flesh." To speak evil of one's spouse is to speak evil of oneself. Marriage ties are weakened, and curses are imposed when a spouse speaks evil of his or her companion.

Early in my life, word curses were inflicted upon me by my father. In my childhood environment, when my emotions and perceptions of life were taking shape, I went to bed angry. It has been proven that the hippocampus-amygdala in the center of the brain can shrink by as much as twenty percent in situations of abuse. These changes in brain structure are associated with events that occurred early in life.

In situations of abuse this impairment can result in schizophrenia and bipolar disorder. In extreme circumstances of abuse, as in the atrocities done to victims of mind control, the mind can actually split into different parts manifesting itself in the form of multiple personalities.

While the abuse I endured wasn't anything like mind control, nonetheless, my environment was stressful at times. Some of my childhood experiences were not positive. I often cried myself to sleep on many occasions resulting in going to bed angry. By going to bed angry,

OUT OF DARKNESS...INTO THE LIGHT

I unknowingly gave place to the devil.

Be ye angry, and sin not; let not the sun go down upon your wrath: Neither give place to the devil.

Ephesians 4:27-28

Demons cannot enter at will; they must have a legal right, or a gateway of opportunity. By letting the sun go down on my wrath, I gave place to the devil and gave him an open door to work in my life.

As a little girl I often wondered, why did I have to suffer so much abuse growing up? All I ever really wanted was to have a normal life and a daddy who loved me. I even began to wonder, if there really is a God. Although deep down I knew there was a God, I just did not realize how close He was to me.

When I was eight years old, I was playing outside in the street on my skateboard. I used to sit on my skateboard in the middle of the street where it was flat and I could roll very slowly. As I rounded the curve on the street where I lived, I would have enough momentum to go flying down the approaching hill.

On one particular afternoon as the sun was slowly setting, I put my skateboard down in the middle of the street where it was flat and sat down upon it. I started rolling very slowly when, all of a sudden, I heard a loud screeching noise coming from behind me. The next thing I heard was a huge crash. It happened so quickly I did not know what had actually occurred. I only knew I was lying in the middle of a ditch across the street from where I had been.

The person in the car had not seen me sitting in the street on my skateboard until too late and had to slam on his brakes to keep from hitting me. His car went

MY CHILDHOOD YEARS

into the ditch across the street from where I had landed. One minute I was in the middle of the street; in the next instant I was in the ditch of our neighbor's front yard. A neighbor who had seen the entire event could not believe her eyes. A force of some kind had literally picked me up out of the street and had safely moved me to keep me from being hit by the car. Everyone was in shock as to how this could have happened. My mother and I both knew God was watching over me and had sent His angel to protect me!

> *For He shall give His angels charge over thee, to keep thee in all thy ways. They shall bear thee up in their hands, lest thou dash thy foot against a stone.*
>
> *Psalms 91:11-12*

In Billy Graham's book entitled *Angels,* he speaks of how angels are watching; they mark our path. They superintend the events of our lives and protect the interest of the Lord God, always working to promote His plans while being about His highest will for us. Angels are interested spectators that mark all we do.

God assigns angelic powers to watch over us. Rev. Graham says each Christian may have his own guardian angel assigned to watch over him or her. This guardianship possibly begins in infancy for Jesus said:

> *Take heed that ye despise not one of these little ones; for I say unto you, That in heaven their angels do always behold the face of my Father which is in heaven.*
>
> *Matthew 18:10*

The near wreck was my first known encounter with the forces of the supernatural world and God at work in my life.

My second encounter involved the death of my great-grandmother, Nannie Up. Nannie Up was the dearest, sweetest lady, much like my mother. Nannie Up loved Jesus and was another great inspiration in my life. She played the organ in her ladies' lodge and for different events.

At Christmas, I loved to hear her play "Silent Night." We would all gather around the organ; she would play and we would sing. Nannie Up always made Christmas a special time at her house. She baked all sorts of good food, from turkey and dressing to the many homemade sweets we enjoyed eating so much. Her chocolate fudge was simply out of this world!

Nannie Up loved to cook for family and friends and enjoyed having people over to her house to eat. At Thanksgiving and Christmas, I would ask the blessing before we would eat; each time after I would say grace, Nannie Up would always close by saying, "Now, darling, that was sweet!"

Nannie was such a lovely lady. Nannie's maiden name was Lee, Annie Lee. Nannie had a lot of history in her family as she was a descendant of General Robert E. Lee. I used to sit and listen to her tell stories of her own childhood. In the summer time when I would run around half-naked in shorts and a skimpy top, she would always scold me. She told me that, when she was a young girl, the most she would show of herself was her ankles, from underneath her petticoat. She said that, back then, that was considered flirting. I thought that was so funny and would laugh so hard at the stories she would tell me.

Nannie Up worried so much about me as a teenager

because she knew of all the abuse I had suffered from my father. She loved my father but did not approve of the way he treated me. She used to tell me, "Now, Laurie, your daddy loves you, and he doesn't mean to lose his temper and act ugly with you. It's just part of his nature. He treats you ugly because his father treated him ugly. He does not know how to give you love because he was never given love himself. In the Bible it says to forgive and forget. So, darling, this is what you must do—love him and forgive him."

I would say, "Okay, Nannie Up, I will try."

I spent summers going to visit her, cutting the grass, raking the yard, and doing whatever chores needed to be done around her house. As a teenager, I would always take my boyfriend of the moment over to meet her. Nannie Up always had to meet and approve of all my boyfriends. We would visit with her and keep her company. As a child, even into my teenage years, I always knew the importance of making my loved ones feel loved and needed.

When Nannie Up got older, into her eighties, we had to sell her car because she could no longer see to drive. Nannie had always been so independent and now being unable to drive made her feel like she was a burden to other members of the family. She would worry and get somewhat upset when she had to ask someone to go out of his or her way for her. She encouraged each of us children to come and visit her when we had time. I loved my Nannie Up dearly and did all I could for her.

One Monday night before Nannie Up died, I was sitting in the den doing my homework. All of a sudden, I had the strangest urging telling me... "Go see your Nannie." It was around 8:30 p.m. I jumped up and ran to the telephone and dialed her number. The phone rang twice and she answered, "Hello."

I said, "Nannie Up, hey, this is Laurie. What are you doing?"

She said, "Oh, Nannie is just sitting here about to go to bed."

I said, "Well, Nannie, listen, I was going to come and visit you this evening."

She replied, "Oh, darling, that's sweet of you, but Nannie is not feeling well this evening; you can come and visit Nannie another time."

I finished my conversation with, "All right, Nannie, I will do that when you are feeling better. I love you, Nannie!" I heard her say, "I love you too, darling."

The next night was Tuesday. Once again I was sitting in the den doing homework when I had the same strange urge coming over me again... "Go see your Nannie." I jumped up and called her, only this time there was no answer. I panicked! I phoned my grandmother, Big Mama and asked, "Where is Nannie Up?"

She said, "Well, honey, she's sitting right here. Would you like to speak with her?"

I frantically said, "Yes!"

Nannie Up took the phone and said, "Hello." I asked her what she had been doing and she said, "Oh, I am just sitting here having dinner with Big Mama and Big Daddy." I told her that I had planned to come over to visit her this evening.

Once again she said, "Well, darling, that is sweet of you, but Nannie is tired and not feeling well this evening and Big Mama is about to take me home. You can come and visit Nannie another time, dear."

I said, "Okay, I will do that. I love you, Nannie!" Her reply was, "I love you too, dear."

The next day, Wednesday, I came home from school and I knew something was very wrong because both my parents were waiting for me, and they were there... together. We walked into the house without speaking a word. The last time they looked at me like this was when my German shepherd had died. My mother finally burst into tears. "Laurie, honey," she sobbed, "Nannie Up passed away peacefully during the middle of the night in her sleep. She died exactly the way she had always wanted to go. She's in heaven now."

I was devastated and so overwhelmed with grief I could not speak. I felt so guilty because for the past two nights I had been given what I now know to be "divine insight" to go and visit with my Nannie before she died and had not done so. I had a chance to say goodbye to her that I felt could never come again.

That evening was very painful for me. I could not bear to be around anyone because I felt so guilty. Family and friends gathered and I just wanted to be left alone. How I missed my Nannie Up. Later that evening, I cried myself to sleep.

Then in the wee hours of the morning it happened. Something woke me from my sleep. A voice said, "Get up! Get up! Laurie, get up!" I thought the voice came from a girlfriend of mine, Pam (not her real name). However, it was the voice of an angel. Suddenly some force propelled me straight up and left me resting gently against the headboard of my bed. My whole bedroom was lit up brighter than the fireworks on the Fourth of July. My entire room was filled with an intensely bright, white light. My whole body was filled with "holy bumps," the kind I get when I feel the Holy Spirit speaking to me, but a thousand times greater.

I asked, "Pam, is that you?" From this moment on, there was no verbal communication made through speaking; it was all done mentally. As I listened intently, the Lord spoke to me in a voice I would recognize.

The voice said, "No, darling, it's Nannie, and Nannie just wanted to tell you before I go that I love you very much and that I know you are not living right. Nannie wants you to change your ways so you can come and join me here one day." She continued, "Tell everyone that I love them and not to be sad about my death; my knee does not hurt anymore and I am not sick. I must go now because I see Pop." Pop was Nannie's husband, who had passed away before I was born.

As quickly as the light came, it left. I was wide awake in total darkness. Again I was pushed straight up and back against my headboard just as I had been when I heard the voice of an angel order me to get up. I cannot describe how peaceful it felt to be in such a divine and holy presence. What a shock it was knowing I had been in the very presence of God and His angels, closer than I had ever been before, and then to return to the total darkness of this world. I felt even more alone, in my world of sin and rebellion.

As Rev. Billy Graham points out in his book *Angels*, "It is not unreasonable to ask, what did they say when they spoke?" In the Bible, angels seemed to communicate terse commands. Often the angels' messages urged haste, and this is understandable since they were communicating a directive from God. The words, "Get up," were sometimes literally used. The angel said to Peter, "Rise quickly." An angel said to Gideon, "Arise and go in this thy might." An angel said to Joseph, "Go quickly," and to Philip, "Arise and go."

I knew at this moment that there is a God. He had spoken just a few final words of comfort to let me know my deceased loved one was at peace in His presence in heaven. Wasn't God wonderful to let me know there is a heaven and to give me just a small taste of it?

The Bible shows that God feels it is an abomination to seek visits from the dead as Saul did in *I Samuel 28:8*, and that we should never call up the dead, *Deuteronomy 18:11*. There have been many Christians with experiences where they did not seek visions from the dead nor did they call them up, but God sovereignly visited them or sanctioned it in one way or another. In *Matthew 17*, Jesus took Peter, James, and John unto a high mountain and was transfigured and Moses and Elijah appeared to them and talked with Jesus. While Jesus was on earth in bodily form, He talked with the dead (Elijah and Moses) as the three disciples witnessed the event. In addition, God the Father blessed Jesus at the time. If this experience were not of God, Jesus would not have participated, and the Father would not have sanctioned it. The disciples did not seek this visit with the dead and God did not criticize it or condemn it, but in fact also talked to them and said, "This is my beloved son in whom I am well pleased." We must never seek visits from the dead or call up the dead. Further, the fact that I had the exact same unction from the Holy Spirit for two nights in a row is symbolic according to scripture.

And for that the dream was doubled unto Pharaoh twice; it is because the thing is established by God, and God will shortly bring it to pass.

Genesis 41:32

For God speaketh once, yea twice.

Job 33:14

Therefore, this experience I had was most certainly Divine. Only God knows the future, and only God knew that He was about to take my Nannie home to Heaven.

The next morning I knew I had experienced something divine. I tried to tell my mother and all of my family members, but they thought I was dreaming. I was so discouraged. All I wanted to do was to share the experience of being in the presence of divine light, but they didn't seem to understand.

Strange as it was, it was only my father who believed me. He told me that, when I was four years old, I said I saw his mother after she died. I woke up in the middle of the night telling him I had seen Grandmother Wallace. I told him she was in heaven. Ironically, my parents had not yet told me of her death when I reported my vision.

Still looking for someone who could fully understand my experience, I went to talk to a friend's mother, LaVerne. She was not the least bit skeptical of my story and, without a doubt, she believed me. LaVerne was a devout Christian and attended a full-gospel church. Her church was having a revival during the week of Nannie's death and she invited me to attend the evening service. Since Nannie's viewing would not be until the next day, I accepted her invitation. At the close of the service, LaVerne and I went down to the front and knelt to pray at the altar. She asked the Lord to give me some guidance and to reveal the purpose for having this experience after Nannie's death.

A few moments later, the pastor's wife joined us at the altar in prayer and held my other hand. The pastor's wife later told LaVerne that the Holy Spirit had led her to get up out of her seat and come to the altar to me. She continued to share with LaVerne that she did not know why the Holy Spirit had led her to take such an action. She only knew that the Holy Spirit was speaking and she acted upon His indwelling Spirit.

LaVerne told me the pastor's wife was very spiritually gifted and her being led to me, not having known me or anything about me, was surely a sign. Later LaVerne told me God was going to do something wonderful with my life. She said, "Laurie, God has a special plan for you. I can just feel it, and it is going to be big!"

Being the troubled teenager I was at this time, I did not fully comprehend what she meant. I knew something marvelous had happened to me, and yet I could not make sense of the experience.

Chapter Two

BECOMING A WOMAN

As I grew older, I always felt there was something very special about me. There were times when I felt close to God, but I had not come into full maturity with God as a Christian.

The impact of my experience after Nannie's death had an effect on my life for awhile, but soon I was back to being my same rebellious self. From the time I was young, I wanted to lash out in anger at my father. I would say to my mother, "I'm going to get him back for you one day. I am going to do things to cause him pain and embarrassment just like he has done to us. Don't you worry; I'll make him pay." My mother remembers with such regret all the times I would say this to her. During this time in my life, I was able to be so good, only to turn and become so bad.

In high school, I stayed in trouble as I skipped school repeatedly. A concerned teacher noticed the changes in my behavior. Mrs. Smith had known me since grammar school because I had always been such an excellent gymnast. Mrs. Smith used to judge some of my gymnastic meets and coached gymnastics where I later attended high school.

Mrs. Smith had always liked me and was concerned when she noticed such a drastic change in my behavior. I created a lot of trouble for myself when I skipped school. Mrs. Smith called my mother and asked her, "What has happened to Laurie? She was such a sweet little girl. What has happened to her?" I had been skipping class so much I failed to take my tests and, as a result, I decided to forge the grades on my report card. Both of my parents were livid with me. My father came and checked me out of school, took me home, and almost beat me to a pulp. Of course, the entire time, my mother was praying for me, praying that my father would not kill me. I must have had belt marks up and down both of my legs for over a month.

Truly, the spirit of rebellion was upon me, not only at school but at home too. At the age of fifteen, I would sneak out during the middle of the night many times, taking my parents' car just to drive around town...until one night when I wrecked it. I can only thank God He was watching over me during these times. I also had another wreck at the age of sixteen. With the deadly combination of drinking and driving, it is amazing I did not kill myself or someone else. I am sure there was a guardian angel around that night too, but I was too drunk to remember. All I remember is waking up in a jail cell with my head pounding and people gazing at me as if I were some sort of criminal.

Much of my teenage years was spent pulling stunts like these and various others that drove my parents crazy. They could not understand what was wrong with me, and neither could I.

The one thing I am proud of is the fact that,

regardless of all the trouble I had been in or caused, I was not promiscuous as others thought. I have always held the philosophy that there are two kinds of girls: those who say they don't, but they really do; and those everyone thinks do, but they really don't. I was the latter, and for a very good reason. My father was notoriously violent. No boy in his right mind would have attempted to do anything with me. (Because of this, I was never faced with making the decision so many of our teenagers are faced with today...abortion.)

When dating, guys would say to me, "You are nothing like you appear to be." I always appeared to be wild as I have always been an extrovert. I have always been one to say exactly what I think. You do not have to wonder where you stand with me because I just come right out and say it. Sometimes this works in my favor and at other times it does not.

I had never studied much in high school, when I attended, and I paid for it dearly by the time I got to college. I had a hard time knowing how to apply myself in my studies because I had never done so in high school. From first grade through the sixth grade, I was an excellent straight "A" student. Then in junior high my grades dropped as my parents' marital problems grew. I had the ability to succeed but not the drive. I was in my own little world, subconsciously rebelling against everything and everybody—even God. I was consumed with the spirit of rebellion.

Distressed and under duress, my mother took me to see a counselor at Campus Life. Although he was nice, I refused to cooperate. I started picking up books off his desk and throwing them at him as hard as I possibly could. After all, I was not the one with the problems, right? Boy, was I ever mistaken!

During that first visit, even after my book-throwing

tantrum, he did eventually get through to me a little bit...at least the second time I went to see him I didn't throw any more books. I actually started to like him. He surmised that my problems were ones deeply rooted in my relationship with my father.

He was right. As I grew older and started to become a young woman, I would fall in and out of love with one man right after the other. It would usually be the ones with whom I became obsessed who would end up hurting me. Mine was the same old story: Woman wants to be loved and feel safe and secure and man wants freedom and his space. Consequently, when a man would pull away, I felt rejected. This really pushed my panic button. I had always searched for a man's love, even my father's, as a child growing up.

When I was in my twenties, still in college, I did not have a serious boyfriend. I was having too much fun. At the age of twenty-three, I found a wonderful substitute for life—before it was made illegal. It was a drug called Ecstasy. This drug was designed for people with marital problems and suffering from inhibitions. This New Age drug was designed to help you "open up." It was often referred to as the "love drug." Most of the people who took it would end up making love all night. However, I was affected in a different way because, when I took it, all I could do was dance all night. I could dance for six or seven hours straight. The music of this era was so beguiling. The music would lure me into a universe where I alone, was the ruler. One song I remember in particular was, **American Soviets by C.C.C.P.** During this era, my generation was being psychologically conditioned to accept the Soviet Union as an ally. We were further being conditioned to willfully accept becoming part of the United Nations to create a New World Order.

Finally, wringing wet with sweat, the drug would start to wear off and I was ready for sleep. By using this New Age drug, I had not realized what I had actually done to my body, mind, and spirit.

During this stage of my life, I had opened myself up to demons, and I was unaware of their presence in my life. Already consumed with the spirit of rebellion, I now damaged my body and spirit with drugs. God does not intend for us to do things that alter the state of our minds. The drug Ecstasy/LSD is a mind-altering drug. Anytime one gives up control of the mind, he is giving that control to something or someone.

This mind-altering drug temporarily consumed my life, feeding me its synthetic lies. You are never aware of the demons you allow to enter your body through altered states of consciousness when using drugs such as Ecstasy, cocaine, alcohol, marijuana, or LSD. Whenever you harm your body, you open yourself up to demons who manifest themselves in your flesh like parasites.

Luckily for me, I quickly grew out of this stage of my life. I reflect back upon it now and wish I had never damaged my body or my spirit in this manner. But instead I had to learn my lesson the hard way. Now I know my body is not mine as it belongs to God and I should have kept it holy for the Bible says:

> *Know ye not that your body is the temple of the Holy Ghost which is in you, which ye have of God, and ye are not your own? For ye are bought with a price: therefore glorify God in your body, and in your spirit, which are God's.*
>
> *I Corinthians 6:19-20*

The nightclub, drugs, and party scene, were no longer holding my interest. During this time of my life, I found myself caught between two different schools of thought. I was trapped between the baby boomers and "Generation X," although I was not even cognizant of what exactly "Generation X" represented. I would describe myself as a woman who had a vision. I seemed to want more out of life than the norm. I was on a quest for something. At this point in my life, I certainly did not understand exactly just what it was that I longed for. I only knew that it was something. During this time of my life, I had yet to find myself. All I knew, is that I was looking for something much different from the adolescent years of my past.

Everything about myself began to subtly change, my interest, my circle of friends, and the people I was attracted to. In my early and mid twenties, I would date men much older than myself. During this time of my life, success, knowledge and power fascinated me. In fact, the more power a man would have, the more interested I was in him. My appeal in men of this caliber was mostly of a mental nature. Men I perceived as highly educated with lots of credentials to hang upon their walls. My standards of judging a person were by only how much they had accomplished in life. This was, indeed, a most shallow time for me.

I guess deep in my heart, I wanted to know love. Maybe this is what I was searching for. I wanted to experience all the things that one would think love to be. Still, much a little girl at heart. I sometimes felt as though I were this little girl, trapped in a woman's body. I suppose I was still looking for a father figure. The father figure I never had.

My relationships with men, in particular, over the years have been rocky. I have always been the type to want whatever I could not seem to have. This is true of all human nature, but probably more true for me.

The men who came into my life that liked me the least little bit, I would have little or no interest in. I have always reached for the unobtainable. I even developed a philosophy about men in general: Men are like parking spaces; all of the good ones are taken.

One would think that, after having seen my mother endure so much pain from my father's affairs, I would never do such a thing, but I did. Four different times within a period of seven years, I had affairs with married men. My fear of commitment kept me from becoming involved with someone available. Also, at an early age I vowed that I would never be like any of those women who destroyed my family. There is a spiritual law at work in this type of situation that works against a single woman who takes a vow.

But every vow of a widow, and of her that is divorced, wherewith they have bound their souls, shall stand against them.

Numbers 30:9

This was the beginning of a pattern for me—a very self-destructive pattern. Because of the vow I had made, there was a spiritual force working against me bringing into my life the very thing I vowed never to do... "Be like any of those women who helped destroy my family." The only thing I was accustomed to was chaos in my life. When I would meet a nice guy and would start to have a "normal relationship" with him, I became bored very quickly and was ready to move on to something more exciting. I know I hurt a lot of nice, innocent men during these years, but "nice" guys bored me. I would constantly rationalize my situation by thinking this relationship is so good and forthright, it is just sickening. I wanted to find a "bad" guy and make him "good." You know the type, the one who treats all women terribly and will lie, cheat, and deceive. I thought I could perform some sort of magic and all of a sudden he would become good. Magic does work, but at this point in my life I had yet to discover how and why, or what the effects and the results would be.

I drifted in and out of relationships, from one heartbreak to another. Although I gave up my virginity, my lovers were few. Once a love affair of mine had ended, it took me well over a year and a half to get over that person. During these times, it would be difficult for me to become involved with someone else.

I have always pined over a lost love, and I feel fortunate not to have contracted AIDS. With the AIDS virus spreading at such a rapid rate, a person cannot be too careful these days. I know it can take years to develop the virus after even one instance of unprotected sex.

I firmly believe we as a society have AIDS because of sin. I believe AIDS is the disease described in the Book of Revelation. I know without a doubt it was wrong for me to have sex outside marriage. The consequences of sin damages the body, mind, and spirit. Once again I had damaged my body and spirit and had opened myself up to demons I was unaware of—that is, of course, until they revealed themselves to me at a much later time in full force.

God gave us sex to be enjoyed within certain boundaries. One of the most beautiful and meaningful relationships two people of the opposite sex can share is the oneness of physical union, properly called "the act of marriage." God meant this experience both for the propagation of the human race and for the emotional enrichment and physical pleasure of husband and wife. Contrary to popular opinion, sex is a sacred and holy experience in the eyes of God when confined to marriage. In fact, the Bible makes it very clear that God considers any form of sex outside the marriage relationship to be a perversion of sex. Also, sex is the only sin you can commit in which you sin against your very own body.

Flee fornication. Every sin that a man doeth is without the body; but he that committeth fornication sinneth against his own body.

I Corinthians 6:18

This Scripture clearly tells us all other sins are committed outside the body, but this is the one sin we commit inside our bodies when we have sex outside marriage. Sex is a powerful high and anyone having a "death wish" can practice it these days outside marriage. Through fulfilling the desires of the flesh, you open yourself up to demons you are unaware of. Most people feel that, if they cannot see something, then it isn't there. We are taught to believe only in visible things. "Seeing is believing," we are told. If we can see it, then it must exist. If we can't see it, it must not exist. However, demons and the damages they inflict are very real.

The consequence of sin is contamination by diabolic forces of evil in endless forms. God loves each of us and He gave the Ten Commandments to us for our protection and for our good. When we disobey God and break one of His laws through sin, we leave a hole in our hedge of protection and the devil then has access to us. I became consumed with a spirit of rebellion, which is as bad as the sin of witchcraft, for the Bible says:

> *For rebellion is as the sin of witchcraft, and stubbornness is as iniquity and idolatry.*
>
> *I Samuel 15:23*

I know I was wrong to engage in such acts as sexual relations outside marriage and drugs because such acts could surely destroy me by death, the wrath of God.

From this sketch of my background, you can begin to see the big picture of my life. There was a time in my life when I loved Jesus very much, so much that I asked Him to come into my heart. A poem I wrote in 1987 about a friend of mine reflects this love:

MY FRIEND

Have you ever had a friend
  that listens to your heart
When you're down and lonely
  and feeling torn apart?

Have you ever had a friend
  that always has time to give,
That meets the purpose of life
  and makes you want to live?

Have you ever had a friend
  that hears your every prayer,
That always knows what you're thinking
  and if you really care?

Have you ever had a friend,
someone whom you could turn to,
Who would not turn and walk away
but somehow help you through?

If you've never had a friend like this,
then I suggest you find out why
Because this friend of mine is Jesus
and without him, my sun won't shine.

I not only loved Jesus when I was young, but I have always loved him throughout my life. Even when I sinned, I still knew what was truly in my heart, and it was the Truth.

And ye shall know the truth, and the truth shall make you free.

John 8:32

Though I believed in Jesus as my Saviour, I had never committed myself to Him and made Him the Lord of my life. I straddled the fence much of my life between good and evil. I rebelled against God for the things I had suffered during childhood. My Christian temperature was lukewarm. I had become neutral. Satan, who is at the root of all sin, will take advantage of anyone who tries to remain neutral.

So then because thou art lukewarm, and neither cold nor hot, I will spue thee out of my mouth.

Revelation 3:16

God spit me right out of His mouth and into a

place from which there is usually no return. Satan gets no greater pleasure than making a Christian, a child of God, stumble and fall. Even though I felt I had been saved and was assured of salvation, I surely was not living in a Christian manner. I had sinned so much, God gave me up to my sin.

> *Wherefore God also gave them up to uncleanness through the lusts of their own hearts, to dishonour their own bodies between themselves:*
>
> *Who changed the truth of God into a lie, and worshipped and served the creature more than the Creator, who is blessed forever. Amen.*
>
> *For this cause God gave them up unto vile affections: for even their women did change the natural use into that which is against nature.*
>
> *And likewise also the men, leaving the natural use of the woman, burned in their lust one toward another; men with men working that which is unseemly, and receiving in themselves that recompence of their error which was meet.*
>
> *And even as they did not like to retain God in their knowledge, God gave them over to a reprobate mind, to do those things which are not convenient;*
>
> *Being filled with all unrighteousness, fornication, wickedness, covetousness, maliciousness; full of envy, murder, debate, deceit, malignity; whisperers.*

Backbiters, haters of God, despiteful, proud, boasters, inventors of evil things, disobedient to parents,

Without understanding, covenant-breakers, without natural affection, implacable, unmerciful:

Who knowing the judgment of God, that they which commit such things are worthy of death...

Romans 1:24-32

Having rebelled so much and being given up to my sin and reprobate mind, I almost destroyed myself. I have truly been to the other side and have experienced the consequences of leading a sinful life.

Chapter Three

SAYING GOOD-BYE

At the age of twenty-six, I moved away from home and all my family. I must admit I had a lot of reservations about taking this step. I had a conversation with a friend of mine, an older woman, who gave me some insight I had never thought of before.

She said, "If you can see yourself walk down the stairs in a million-dollar ball gown, it can happen. If you can see it in your mind, it can happen." I had never seen things in this light before, and something just clicked in my mind. I then realized I had actually done this all my life. I had used creative, mental visualization. I had created pictures in my mind for every single thing I had ever accomplished. I was amazed at hearing this because, until that moment, I had been totally unaware of what I had been doing.

One of Satan's biggest enticements is to get you to seek your will instead of God's. Satan's great deception is to get you to affirm that anything the human mind can believe, the human mind can achieve.

I moved to Houston, Texas, after I had visualized

the move for three months. I chose Houston because it was the largest city not too far from home. After college, I was so sick of living in a small town I would have pulled my hair out if I had had to stay there any longer. My mother had also moved away to another state when she had remarried.

I was ready for this big move, one that would promise to be exciting. Once I made up my mind to move, I flew to Houston, checked into the Four Seasons Hotel, and bought a newspaper. After five days I landed a job and returned home to pack my things.

My brother, David, and sister, Rebecca, and I had been very much at odds during my years at home, mostly due to my bad temper and my rebellious and stubborn ways. During my teenage years, I was not really close to either of them. We constantly fought with each other, and I am sure they disliked me at one time or another. However, I became close to the two of them before I moved to Houston. Before I left, my baby sister wrote me the sweetest letter:

Laurie:

> *Gosh, where do I begin or what do I say to you at a time like this? I really regret us not being so close as we should have been these past years. I really hate goodbyes, but I know it's not for good. The way I cope with these types of things is to wipe them out of my mind like for instance when mom left I tried to forget about her cause I could not face it that she remarried and was gone.*
>
> *Today, I still have trouble with it because I miss her so bad. I hope you will one day realize how much you mean to me and the rest of the family. We have all*

had our ups and downs but we have managed. Somehow God has made each and every one of us survivors.

I know we have not seen much of each other or even talked but I see how close you and David have become and it hurts me. Pretty stupid. I bet you are thinking? Well, you see there is a big gap between my age and ya'lls. I guess what I am trying to come out and say is I am jealous. A lot of things that concern you make me jealous and I know I should not be like that.

I cannot seem to face the fact that you are going to be gone. I wish I could block it all out. I do not see holidays and other things without you! There have been so many times when I was hurting and upset that I wanted to call you and look for help but I could not let you know or lead you to realize how insecure a person I really am.

I look up to you for your bravery because I know I could never have the courage to do something like you are about to do. I know that as you leave you are scared half to death, but I know that you can handle and accomplish anything that comes to pass you by. Mainly, because you are a survivor and when you set your mind to it, you can do just about anything.

You know I wish you the best in everything you do and I hope to hear from you frequently. So please do not forget about your baby sister who <u>loves you so very much</u>!

One day we will be together again I hope, because I do not think I can handle two long distance relationships for the rest of my life. Do not worry, I will go see Big Mama and Big Daddy. But Good Luck and I am praying that everything will go for the best. Just be careful and think positive about everything you may come to face.

I Love You ! ! !
Rebecca

P.S. "I can do all things through Christ who strengthens me."

Philippians 4:13 — Memorize it!

Tears streamed down my face as I read her letter. My sister, Rebecca, is an absolute angel for she is truly a "miracle baby." She looks a lot like me, but she is even more beautiful. She too has long blonde hair, lovely blue eyes, and the cutest little turned-up nose. She stands about 5'4" tall and weighs, at most, 110 pounds. She is an absolute doll and how I have always loved her.

I had fought with my brother, David, for many years and we both were at odds with each other for such a long time, but we had become very good friends before I left and realizing how close we were made my move very difficult. He wrote:

Laurie:

I just want you to know that I love you very much. I hope that you will be happy with your new life. I know in the past we really were not close. But in the past months, I felt like we have grown really close. I have felt that I could really come to you with all my problems when I had no one to turn to.

I want you to know that I have had a blast hanging out with you. You are so much fun to be around, and I hope to do it again. I wish that we had spent more time together. I am really going to miss you and I hope you know that I love you very much!

Your Brother and Friend,
David

My father and I had also made amends. I took Nannie Up's advice and forgave him for the anguish he had caused my family over the years.

Judge not, and ye shall not be judged: condemn not, and ye shall not be condemned: forgive, and ye shall be forgiven.

Luke 6:37

I forgave my father and I persisted in showing him love. Can you guess what happened? Over the years, my father changed. He is not the same person he once was; he is a better person. As hard as he was on me during my growing-up years, he taught me something I could never have learned on my own without his guidance...how to be a survivor! Despite the abuse, I know now he always loved me dearly in his heart as I was his first, most precious child.

I can remember a little dance routine I would do for him before the abuse began. After he had come in from a hard day at work, I would dance and sing, "Roses on my shoulders; slippers on my feet; I'm my daddy's darling; don't you think I'm sweet." I would then jump into his arms and kiss him on the cheek. Those were happy days!

The hardest part of moving was leaving all my family behind. I shall never forget the day I left. My father and I drove off in a big U-haul with my worldly goods inside. We stopped at my grandparents' house just before we left and said our tearful good-byes. I owe them a debt of gratitude for the way they enriched my life.

Now my father and I would begin on a new adventure and make new memories. We spent fifteen hours together on the long trip from the small town where I lived in Alabama to Houston, Texas. We used this time to repair our damaged relationship and find forgiveness. We talked for hours and started our healing process.

My father apologized for all the pain he had caused during the previous years. He said the pressures in his life caused him to behave the way he had. He admitted that divorcing my mother was the biggest mistake of his life. He said he still loved my mother, and always would, yet he wished her the best of everything with her new husband. He said he wanted her to have all the love she deserved, love he could never give her. Even today, a part of me still wishes they could be together and we could be a family again.

Then it was my turn. I apologized for being a spoiled brat and getting into trouble. I tried to explain why I had done some of the many things I had done. I told him how, from the time I was little, I had always said I would get him back for the things he had done to us. And I knew now I had only hurt myself in the process.

The conversation we had with one another was almost as healing as going to therapy, for both of us. I shall always cherish this time we had to make amends for the many bad years between us.

My father wrote me a letter after I had settled into my new apartment:

Dear Laurie:

I guess you have by now gotten settled in. I got a call from my insurance company on Friday, that they were paying the claim on the wrecker service. So you don't have to marry a millionaire to repay me. How are you doing with your job?

Are you meeting a lot of new people? Rebecca is about to start college. David is still doing fine, although he would like to get out on his own...it will probably be awhile.

Laurie, I am glad that I got a chance to go with you to Houston, as it was quite an experience. I just want you to know that I do love you very much and I hope the best for you in Houston. You take care of yourself and do get plenty of rest. I have thought a lot in the last two weeks about you!

*Love always,
Your Father*

For both of us, the trip to Texas was an experience we will never forget. We laughed, we cried, and we got stuck in the mud in Lafayette, Louisiana, in the middle of the dead, hot summer! We had to get a tow truck with a crane attached to it to pull us out. And did I forget to mention that we were almost eaten alive by mosquitos? On July 1, 1991, we finally arrived at the apartment I had chosen a week earlier to live in. Houston, Texas, would be my new home.

Chapter Four

HOW I WAS ENTICED

At last I was on my own in the big city. After moving to Houston, I went to work at a law firm as a legal secretary. This was not my long-term plan, but I thought it would allow me to decide whether or not I liked living in Houston and whether or not I would stay.

My father called me from time to time to see how I was doing. He expected me to return home after a few months. After all, this was the first time I had ever been away from my family and out on my own. He just knew I would be too homesick. He would tease me and say, "You will be back before you know it. I'm just glad you did not move all the way to California."

He was right; I did get homesick. Once I was all settled in my new home, I realized I was all alone in a big, strange city and I knew not one person. I thought to myself, "What on earth have I done?"

It took me almost a year to find my way around Houston. I remember the first few months every single time I would get on Loop 610, which is a freeway that circles the city of Houston for miles, I would get lost and end up in the middle of what I'd call "Estaboga," meaning only God knows where you are at the time. I would stop at a gas station to ask for directions only to hear someone say, "No speak English."

I would say, "What do you mean you do not speak English?"

"No speak English?"

Then, of course, the brave person that I am, I would start crying like a lost, little girl. Eventually, someone would come along and help me. I finally would find my way back to where I lived, but it was certainly not my home.

In the first few months, I came close to calling my father and saying, "Come and get me." I had always had a number of friends back home and found it to be quite difficult those first few months making friends in Houston. All of my friends in Alabama were like me or at least what I perceived myself to be, pretty on the inside and pretty on the outside. In Houston, it was different; many girls who looked like me would turn out to be a dancer in a nightclub or a stripper. I guess if I had been looking in the right places to meet nice people, I might have found some, but unfortunately I did not allow myself that kind of opportunity.

My mom would call me and say, "Honey, how are you doing? Are you meeting a lot of nice people and making new friends?" She also had left home when she remarried and knew what it felt like to leave your home, your roots, and your family.

Mother would send me little cards to perk me up, just to let me know she was thinking of me, as always. But I was still lonely. I must have had a phone bill of no less than $300 per month the first year I lived in

Houston! I called all my family and friends much of the time. But I put on a front and acted as though I was having the time of my life and refused to let any of them know just how homesick I really was. My mother suggested I find a church to start attending, but this was not what I wanted to do. Even though I thought about it, I never took the initiative to follow through with her suggestion until much later.

Having a lot of excess time on my hands and very few friends, I suddenly found myself becoming a bookworm. The books that captivated my interest and excited me were the ones dealing with the power of the subconscious mind, which my friend had suggested to me before I moved to Houston. "If you can see it happen, it can happen." Little did I know this well-meaning advice would position me on a downward spiral from which only the grace of God would save me.

I became very interested in all I read about and the things you could train your mind to do. My favorite topics were "The Magic of Believing" and "The Magic of Thinking Big," which only reaffirmed that there was not anything in this world I could not do. The universe was abundant and everything in it was within my reach. It was this thirst for knowledge and power that led me down the path of destruction.

During my first year in Houston, I worked for a female lawyer I will call Anna. When I interviewed for the job, I subdued my appearance. I wore my hair up in a bun and very little makeup. Shortly after I was hired, I let the real me emerge. My hair came down and the changes were noticed. As Anna walked by my desk one day, she said, "Can I ask you something?"

I said, "Sure."

She proceeded to say, "You didn't look like this when I hired you; you looked different."

I replied, "Oh, really?" and let it go at that, but the whole time I was thinking, "Surprise!" I had been afraid if I appeared too pretty, she would not hire me, but I was not going to tell her that.

Our law firm had two offices downtown. Anna and I were in one office and everyone else was in another office. Anna's boss, Alec (not his real name) was handsome, charming and, of course, married. It became obvious to everyone that he had a secret agenda for me. I was trying so hard not to allow history to repeat itself and he certainly was making it difficult for me. I played the role of the quiet, submissive type for awhile, but it was evident there was chemistry between us.

Between the two offices, he was surrounded by nothing but women. Many times Alec would take all of us out to lunch. He would take us to the most elegant restaurants and most of the conversations would be directed towards me. I am sure the other women at the table felt as though they were not even there. During the entire lunch, Alec and I would stare at one another and you could see the sparks flying.

I tried my hardest not to fall for him, but I just could not help myself. Alec was everything I had searched during my whole life for and, now that I found him, he was not available. He was so kind and generous towards me. I had worked for him less than three months and I decided it was time for a raise. So guess what? I got one. Six months later, I decided it was time for another one. He could not justify it on paper without raising eyebrows, so he had to give everyone a raise just to suit me. I thought, "Now this is a man after my own heart."

With this new interest, even though I was not involved with him at this time, I finally started to like Houston and found myself not being as homesick. I loved to go to work because I knew at some point in the day I would catch a glimpse of his beautiful, blue eyes. I lived for going to work!

In the months that followed, I met his wife, who was also an attorney, at our Christmas party. By then she had heard all about Alec's new employee from Alabama and her dislike for me was apparent. She saw me as a threat to their already troubled marriage, and I suppose I was.

Finally the office gossip became unbearable. Even though everyone thought we were having an affair, we certainly were not. But it was obvious to everyone we were quite fond of each other. Alec was truly my very first love. I do not think I have ever loved another man as much as I did him.

After living in Houston for a year, in July of 1992, I decided to get into medical sales and used my creative visualization to pull this off. I imagined myself making sales calls and talking with doctors. Having had no previous experience and entering the sales force with virtually no sales background, I landed the job!

I found my position in medical sales to be more than I had anticipated. I had a great deal to learn about the anatomy of the body and even more about the products I was selling. I spent many nights reading and trying to learn as much as possible. It seemed as though there were not enough hours in the day to accomplish everything I was faced with.

Alec and I had lunch on July 3, 1992, and this was when we became physically involved with one another. Lunch at La Griglia Restaurant ended up turning into more than I had anticipated. That afternoon, I got on an airplane to go visit my mother for the Fourth of July. The entire time I was there, I stayed on cloud nine. I returned to Houston and Alec had already phoned.

I called his office and left word for him to call me. He told me after this that he needed to work on his marriage and he had set a deadline in his mind—until the end of the year—for it to work. I was very upset, but what could I do? I threw myself into my work to escape some of the pain.

However, by the end of October our paths crossed again. I enticed him once more, and the whole affair started again. I spent Thanksgiving in Temple, Texas, that year because my brother and his fiance were going to be there visiting some of her relatives. I came back a day early and Alec had called me from New Orleans. He left his number where I could reach him at the La Meridian Hotel. I returned his call and he informed me he had to argue a case before the 11th Circuit Court on Monday morning. When he invited me to join him for the weekend, I immediately grabbed some clothes and headed for the airport.

I arrived at the hotel and was so excited to see him that I was literally jumping with joy. We went out for an evening on the town. With so much culture, New Orleans can be such a fun city. The next day, we visited many of the different shops and art galleries. My favorite shop was Dyansen Galleries as they had an entire collection from the artist Erté. I have always been quite fond of this collection and would love to own one of each work if I could afford it.

We walked the streets of New Orleans all day long. We shopped and talked and then we would rest for awhile, then shop some more. He bought me the cutest, little, black dress as a belated birthday present. He kept telling me how things were going to be different after the first of the year, indicating it would be a lot easier for us to see one another as he was planning to leave his wife.

HOW I WAS ENTICED

I left Alec in New Orleans and came back to Houston on Sunday night. On Monday, I had to leave for San Antonio. At this time I was working for a medical company and was being trained on some new equipment by Cindy, a former nurse. During this week, Cindy and I were going down to the Valley, close to Mexico, to work.

We were in Harlingen, Texas, the first week of December. After Cindy and I worked all day, we had dinner and went to the mall to shop for Christmas presents. I found my way into the bookstore as usual. I was very tired and not paying much attention to the time, and before I knew it, Cindy was urging me to hurry up as it was getting late. I had to have something to read, so I grabbed some books that had caught my eye entitled, *Love Codes, How to Marry the Man of Your Choice,* and *Love Magic.* I carelessly did not open any of the books at the time to see what their contents were because Cindy was rushing me and telling me the mall was about to close.

I paid for the books and we left the store. When we arrived at our hotel room, we talked for awhile and laughed about some of the things we had encountered during the day. The main reason we were so tired was that we had been in surgery since 5:00 a.m. with some doctors who were evaluating our equipment.

We laughed about the things that had gone wrong with the equipment and planned our strategy for closing the sale the next day. I was very tired and wanted to go to sleep. In fact, I was so tired I could not go to sleep. I picked up the stack of books I had purchased and started to flip through each one. I glanced through the first two, reading a little bit. Then, I picked up the book entitled *Love Magic.* I opened it and much to my surprise it was nothing more than a book of love spells.

I mean love spells...witchcraft, page after page after page. I had never in my life looked upon anything like this before. I had such an uneasy feeling come upon me; my heart felt so heavy and burdened as my spirit of discernment was cautioning and alerting me not to look upon such a thing as this. I knew then what I was reading was wrong, but I could not put it down. The spells that appealed to me the most were "how to make a man fall in love with you" and "how to separate a man from his wife."

I found my mind so curious, knowing all along that it was wrong for me to read this book's contents. It was as if something were holding my hand to the book. It was this book, reading the contents, that literally pulled me in deeper. Later that night, I had the worst, most terrifying nightmare of my life. I sat straight up in my bed screaming at the top of my lungs as if something had come and manifested itself inside me...and it had. I screamed so loud, I scared poor Cindy half to death. Afterwards, I started crying and trying to explain to her how different I felt and how I had never experienced a nightmare like this before.

She did her best to comfort me and help me go back to sleep. I was so afraid I convinced her I would need to sleep with the bathroom light on. The rest of the night I trembled with fright. I was unaware, until much later, that I had opened myself up to Satan and evil by what I had looked upon and read. They found their way into the very depths of my sinful soul and would not let go.

You may think it odd that a book called *Love Magic* could lead me even further astray, but it did. I had already been dabbling with New Age books. In fact, all of the books I had been reading were New Age. What I read in *Love Magic,* you can find in a magazine or a newspaper today. The nightmare I had was only a glimpse into my future and all that was yet to come. From this moment on, my life has never been the same!

Chapter Five

DABBLING WITH THE OCCULT

I spent the next month away from Alec. When I returned to Houston, it was only a few days before Christmas and time to leave for Alabama, where I was to spend the holidays. I did not see Alec during December.

When I returned from Alabama, we again met to have lunch at La Griglia. I knew for certain he was going to tell me he was leaving his wife for me. This was what I had expected to hear. However, this was not the case. Much to my surprise, he told me something I was not prepared to hear….his wife was pregnant.

I was in such shock I almost dropped my wine glass on the floor. Tears came streaming down my face. I cried out, "No, this cannot be!" I got up from the table and ran into the bathroom. The pit of my stomach felt as if I had just had the breath knocked out of me. He sent someone in to check on me.

I wiped my face and went to sit back down at our table. I looked at him and said, "She's lying; she is making this up to try to trap you and keep you from leaving her." I knew his wife was anything short of naive. They already had one child together, a son. She knew he had always wanted another child, but over the years she had problems conceiving. She knew getting pregnant would be the only way to save their marriage.

I was so sick to my stomach I could not even eat. We left there together and went back to my apartment. I just laid on his chest, crying and sobbing. I really do not think he expected me to take the news in this manner since he had never seen this side of me. I think my reaction sort of scared him. This event triggered a panic button in me that was at the root of my problem with men, saying, "Daddy, please do not leave me!" I continued to lay in his arms for some time before he got up and left. I knew in my heart his wife couldn't be pregnant, and later I found out she had not been. Even so, he still did not leave her because they had decided to go ahead with their plans to build their dream house.

Many months passed and I was not myself. I was deeply hurt. Not a single day went by that I did not think of him or long for him. Our ties to each other caused our relationship to develop such tension that he would no longer talk to me.

At this time, I still possessed *Love Magic*, and something within me had definitely changed. Though I did not realize it, I had opened myself up to Satan and his evil demon spirits and was giving them an incredible amount of power over me. I knew nothing about the occult or the dangers that curiosity could bring to the unwary, unknowing soul. Evil spirits took full advantage of my ignorant mind. The spirits to which I had opened myself were spirits of confusion, spirits of depression, spirits of hatred, and even more spirits of rebellion.

Having grown up in the bible belt and having attended a Baptist church, I knew better than to look upon such evil as this. Already having a special interest in the metaphysical realm concerning powers of the mind, I realized almost too late that this was just another avenue through which Satan could take control of my life. I had always heard we use only 10 percent of our minds, so what could my curiosity possibly hurt? After all, God gave us a mind. Surely he meant for us to expand our knowledge any way we could, I reasoned.

I started searching for answers. For at least a year I was consumed with curiosity and fascination with the occult. I bought book after book on the subject. It seemed as though I could not get my hands on enough books about creative visualization, how to unleash the powers of your subconscious mind, meditation, and even witchcraft—all of which I found at a later time in my life are nothing more than tools with which to obtain the object of *your* desires, or *your* will.

The occult in earlier days was privileged information for only the select few. Now with the New Age Movement upon us, witchcraft and the occult are leisure reading for the masses. New Age is nothing but the Old Age, just packaged differently. And New Age has no boundaries because Satan wants to deceive as many people as he can through this movement.

I could very easily have turned my entire apartment into a bookstore for I had bought so many books on this subject, they were everywhere. Books, meditation tapes, candles, incense, you name it—my home looked and virtually was an occult shop. I even felt it necessary to hide much of this material before I would allow outsiders into my home for fear of what they might think. All of these various forms of the occult had consumed me. I had so much evil in my apartment, it is a wonder I am alive today. I had used creative visualization unknowingly all of my life. Many people believe creative visualization is a goddess-given ability. They teach that all thought is energy, and it is the focused, harnessed, concentrated energy that can bring to manifestation the object of your desires.

I now realize why it is so very important to guard our thoughts and the power of our words. If we only knew the awesome power of our words, we definitely would prefer silence to saying or thinking anything negative.

Much of my spare time was devoted to reading whatever I could possibly get my hands on. Suddenly, I got a brainstorm to take my quest just one step further. You can guess where this idea came from. The Bible teaches us that, if something is not of God, it is of something else. If it does not line up with the Word of God, then it certainly is not of God. My apartment was filled with material of something else. I looked in the Yellow Pages for the word "occult," along with "occult shops and supplies." In Houston, there were at least five listed in the Yellow Pages.

No sooner had I looked up the word "occult" than I enrolled in some classes to take metaphysics. Now keep in mind my religious upbringing in the Baptist church in Alabama. I would have to say I certainly had fallen by the wayside and gotten off my godly path. In fact, I had strayed extremely far away...almost too far! The first few classes seemed rather slow since I was so eager actually to be able to perform some awesome magic trick.

I was enrolled in the basic classes where I learned the Seven Universal Laws. Each of these laws you must know and understand in order for your magic to work.

My teacher, I will call him Jim, was brought up in the Jewish faith though he had been practicing magic or Wicca for very many years. Jim was the owner of the occult shop where our classes were held. We met every Thursday, from 7:00 until 9:00. Jim seemed to be a very nice, intelligent person. In teaching the classes, he made me think of things I had never thought of before concerning the universe. Some of the ideas he would teach I readily accepted. For example, a stick you find on the side of the road is just that, a stick. But if you go out into the woods and find yourself a tree, cut a stick from the tree, and thank the tree for letting you take a piece of it, now you have something more. You have a tool for magic! With this newly acquired tool, you would wait until a night when the moon is full and dedicate it to the moon. Now you have something even more. You now have a magic wand with all the energy you have put into it. In this manner you can empower all the tools you use in magic.

God made the universe and all the things therein. He made the moon, the sun, and the stars above. He made all the trees and flowers, and we are instructed, and even warned, that we are not to worship anything but God Himself. We are to worship God, giving thanks to Him and Him alone for it says in the Scriptures:

> *If there be found among you, within any of thy gates which the Lord thy God giveth thee, man or woman, that hath wrought wickedness in the sight of the Lord thy God, in transgressing his covenant, and hath gone and served other gods, and worshipped them, either the sun, or moon, or any of the host of heaven, which I have not*

commanded; and it be told thee, and thou hast heard of it, and inquired diligently, and, behold, it be true, and the thing certain, that such abomination is wrought in Israel:

Deuteronomy 17:2-4

At the time of my involvement in the occult, I did not know about this Scripture in the Bible that forbids this sort of idolatry. Nor did I realize that, in dedicating something to the moon, I was actually worshiping something else, and something else is always Satan. There is no gray area...God is very clear on this subject. No one can serve two gods:

No man can serve two masters: for either he will hate the one, and love the other; or else he will hold to the one, and despise the other. Ye cannot serve God and mammon.

Matthew 6:24

Even when putting your faith in yourself, you are putting faith in something else. That something else is always Satan! The reason is that, when you put your faith in something else, you are giving Satan permission to be in your life and this only reaffirms the position the devil has with you from the beginning of time, since Adam and Eve.

The philosophy of the New Age is that man is neither sinful nor evil because evil does not exist, and we are capable of being the god of own lives. The deception is in the belief that the human race is evolving toward godhood for the millennial kingdom. By the year 2000,

New Agers think we will be like God. This is the oldest trick in the world. Satan tempted Eve in the garden by telling her she would become as God:

> *And the serpent said unto the woman, "Ye shall not surely die: For God doth know that in the day ye eat thereof, then your eyes shall be opened, and ye shall be as gods, knowing good and evil."*
>
> *Genesis 3:4-5*

I had a hard time accepting the statement Jim made when he said Jesus was only a prophet. Jim knew I was a Christian and made it very clear I did not have to accept his views or thinking on the subject matter. He said I could still keep my views and beliefs that Christ was my Saviour and maybe I would find that magic was not for me. Oh, how I wish I had listened to him!

Jim stated that magic was not for everyone. Some find magic very rewarding and others do not. It just depends on the person. In Wicca, there is no Satan. They do not acknowledge Satan as being anything or anyone. Wicca is classified as "white magic," used for good means or purposes.

Everything in Wicca is good—or so I was told. The goddesses and gods they worship, set up altars and dedicate things to are the idols of the Old Testament. I do not know how on earth I could have been so senseless to even be listening to any of this contamination that was filling my mind with beliefs different from those I originally, as a child, had committed myself to. But again "something" kept whispering in my ear, "You are not doing anything wrong. There is nothing wrong with your curiosity. You are just exploring other realms of religion." I did not know it then, but I do know it now: I had demon spirits all around me who were whispering thoughts into my mind, making me think it was me talking the entire time. The Bible says:

> *Thou shalt have no other Gods before me. Thou shalt not make unto thee any graven image, or any likeness of any thing that is in heaven above, or that is in the earth beneath, or that is in the water under the earth: Thou shalt not bow down thyself to them, nor serve them: for I the Lord thy God am a jealous God, visiting the iniquity of the fathers upon the children unto the third and fourth generation of them that hate me.*
>
> *Exodus 20:3-5*

Any object that purports to give supernatural guidance violates this commandment for the Scriptures teach we should look to the true God alone for direction in our lives. Ouija boards, horoscopes, fortunetellers, and dozens of other such practices violate this basic principle. These practices are a substitute for faith in the living God. For those who disregard this stark warning and make contact with occult spirits, there will be terrible and certain repercussions in the form of sickness, misery, insanity, and sometimes even an early death.

Within the occult, some practices are more deleterious, more dangerous spiritually, physically, and emotionally. For instance, astrology is certainly a dangerous practice but nowhere nearly as dangerous as Satan worship.

Within the range of occultic practices, things that should be looked upon as spawning demonic intervention include astrology, the use of Ouija boards, consulting mediums, engaging in seances, practicing fortunetelling or consulting fortunetellers, using tarot cards, holding to reincarnation doctrines, belonging to Eastern religions that accept Christ as a prophet but not as divine *(I John 4:1-3),* consulting curanderos, voodoo, palmistry, numerology, metaphysics, reading tea leaves, Santaria, cultic practices, Cabala, being the victim of a hex or curse or employing one against others—to name only a few.

Jim would lead us through guided meditations in an attempt to meet our "spirit guides." These guides were to be nice, peaceful, loving guides, who were to be our friends and were there only for our benefit to assist us with our daily life. He would tell the class to imagine seeing our spirit guides coming alongside of us. Once we saw our spirit guide, we were to invite him in. How horrid to know this now! Many people from all religions are getting involved with transcendental meditation; it is everywhere. The spirit guides that people are inviting inside of them are nothing more than demons from Satan. It horrifies me to think what is happening in the world today and people just do not realize what they are getting themselves involved with.

The basic rule remains: Either you invite Jesus into your heart or you invite something else in. People today entertaining such practices are inviting the devil right into them and they do not even realize it. If you have been saved, meaning that at some point in your life you invited Jesus Christ into your heart and accepted Him as your personal Lord and Saviour, you have a promise of eternal life. Having accepted Christ into my heart, I had Jesus living in my spirit. We, like God, have three parts as God created man in His image—Father, Son, and Holy Spirit. Our three parts are spirit, body, and soul. Our soul and spirit are two different things. Our soul is made up of three parts—mind, will, and emotions. I already had Jesus living in my spirit, but I gave the devil the rights to my mind, will, and emotions.

Since I had completed the first phase of classes, I decided to go my own way. I had had enough of being around people who believed all that was being taught. Keep in mind that I still felt I was not doing anything wrong. In my mind, I was only exploring different areas of religion. But my first clue should have been when the teacher said there was no such thing as Satan, Jesus was not the Son of God, and in their religion the pagan deities they worshiped and called Mother Goddess and Father God were good.

My second clue should have been when the teacher advised for mandatory reading a book on psychic self-defense. Psychic self-defense is a practice in which you envision yourself surrounded in a blue, luminous light. You see your entire self in a capsule where no harm can befall you and nothing can get to you. Basically, you are protected from negative energies.

The terms "positive and negative energies" were referred to quite a bit. In magic, you do not work with "spirits," you work with "energies"—different name, same thing. I believe when we're taught the universal laws and recognize there are both positive and negative influences in the world, we have the access to power far beyond our human understanding. When we break one of those laws, going against natural law and order, we have sinned and drawn evil spirits to us.

There are visible and invisible forces at work in this world. God has sovereign control over these forces

DABBLING WITH THE OCCULT

until we go against His will. Once we go against God's will, He can only permit the devil to afflict us. A creature cannot successfully rebel against the creator.

> *For by him were all things created, that are in heaven, and that are in earth, visible and invisible, whether they be thrones, or dominions, or principalities, or powers: all things were created by him, and for him.*
>
> *Colossians 1:16*

We were told to read the book on psychic self-defense and practice it daily.

By now you should really know me, so you know I asked the teacher why, if what we were learning and trying to do was good, was there a need to protect ourselves.

His reply was vague, "...Because there are booger bears out there."

I thought, "Okay, booger bears... Where are they? Who are they? I do not see any booger bears anywhere." Little did I know what was in store for me.

Jim said once you get into magic, you become more open to things. Again, I said to myself, "Open to what things?" I now know what he meant, but I learned the hard way. God has given each of us a hedge of protection. God has given us this protection to guard our thoughts and our minds. When we open ourselves up to Satan and his demons, whether it be through meditation, channeling, contacting spiritual guides, involvement with the occult, or simply through sin and not obeying God's Ten Commandments, we are no longer under God's full divine protection and Satan has access to us.

Particularly I would like to caution you about meditation. Meditation, as taught by the New Age, is a process of emptying all thoughts from your mind. Meditation is a very peaceful, relaxing exercise, but I do not know of any place in the Bible where God advises us to empty all thoughts from our minds. In fact, we are to keep our minds filled with godly thoughts to guard our minds constantly. We are to meditate in prayer and in the Word of God. The definition of meditate according to Webster's Dictionary means to engage in thought or contemplation; to reflect; continued thought.

Another problem I had with meditation was that, once I had emptied all thoughts from my mind, I would then be in a receptive mode to receive communication from a higher intelligence. This is what is frequently referred to as "auto suggestion." Jim told us not to be alarmed or frightened by anything we might hear or see, that we should just go with it, experience it, and accept it. In doing this, I was falling into agreement with demonic forces as this Scripture in the Bible warns:

Can two walk together, except they be agreed?

Amos 3:3

By allowing my mind to sink into the abyss of altered states of consciousness through meditation and visualization, I ignorantly turned over the control of my mind to Satan. The New Age practice of occult meditation leaves the individual in a semiconscious trance state and easily susceptible to influence by demonic spirits. The danger of Eastern meditation by "emptying oneself out" is that, once you've emptied your mind, it can easily be filled up by unholy spirits, which are nothing more than demons from satan.

Jim did warn me that all magic is serious business, "Do what thou will, as long as you harm no one." Are you starting to get the idea now with cue words like "thou will" which means "my will." The whole time, I was learning how to practice and project "my will, my will be done." My sole purpose for dabbling with magic and the occult was for one reason and one reason only: to separate Alec from his wife and to cause them to divorce.

Still, I had convinced myself I was doing no wrong. I was only trying to broaden my skills and sharpen the mind God gave me. I kept saying, "God, you gave me a mind. Surely you want me to learn how to use it, right?" And still "something else" kept whispering in my ear, "You are not doing anything wrong." Because of my unrepented sin, I had strong delusions in my mind. I could not separate right from wrong, and I certainly could not make the right choices. I kept justifying my actions only to become more deeply involved along a path that leads to destruction and often death.

Because of my religious convictions, I could never perform magic like you might think it would be performed—like the super New Agers. I never performed magic in a sacred space or circle, and I never performed magic using any of the tools I had learned about. I "only" dabbled with magic.

I could read a spell out of a book or get creative and make up my own. Making up my own spells seemed to take longer. Eventually, though, I was able to separate Alec from his wife through my creative visualization.

My teacher had warned me that doing a manipulative love spell would be a form of black magic and that to manipulate the free will of another human being was not right. He stated that whatever I sent forth to others would return to me three-fold, but of course I did not listen to him.

I continued with my practices, bringing into manifestation "my will" in the material world. Jim was right. To manipulate the free will of another human being is wrong. The universe God created was designed to function under a system of laws: natural, physical laws and spiritual laws. God has given each of us our own free will and even God does not manipulate our free will. We are given the choice either to place our trust and faith in God or to place it in "something else." I carelessly chose something else. At the time I chose me, "my will," Laurie's will be done, or so I thought.

Those of us who know the Bible, know that Satan, himself, is a fallen angel. Satan fell from heaven because he wanted "his will" instead of God's will. He was cast down from heaven for this reason:

> *How art thou fallen from heaven, O Lucifer, son of the morning! how art thou cut down to the ground, which didst weaken the nations! For thou hast said in thine heart, I will ascend into heaven, I will exalt my throne above the stars of God: I will sit also upon the mount of the congregation, in the sides of the north: I will ascend above the heights of the clouds; I will be like the most High.*
>
> *Isaiah 14:12-14*

Satan was not satisfied with being subordinate to God; he wanted to be all powerful. It is the "I will" or "my will" spirit which is the spirit of rebellion.

In the world of New Age and wanting to learn how

to use the powers of the subconscious mind and casting a high imagination, we are exerting our own free will to obtain power. God does allow it to happen.

In Genesis, Chapter Eleven, when the children of Israel built the tower of Babel, whose top was to reach unto heaven; the children of men were casting a high imagination. From that day forth when the Lord came down to see the city and the tower they had built, He said:

> *...And now nothing will be restrained from them which they have imagined to do.*
>
> *Genesis 11:6*

So you see, when we are outside the Will of God for our lives and determined to do things *our* way, the Lord often permits it. The problem is, it may not be God's best for us, but He can allow it to happen.

With my rebellious nature and having turned to witchcraft and occultism, He allowed it to happen to me. Looking back at my life and realizing just how much I had sinned against God and how I had separated myself from Him, I am blessed to still be alive. There are some "things" that inquiring minds do not need to know. There are things you must simply leave unanswered and ask God about later. In this world, we must live by faith:

> *So then faith cometh by hearing, and hearing by the word of God.*
>
> *Romans 10:17*

I continued with my spiritual journey, practicing

the powers of my mind. There is nothing wrong with positive thinking or positive affirmation or seeking a better state whether it be a new job, new car, or new home. God wants us to prosper...but we are to seek Him first and He will fulfill the desires of our hearts according to His will:

> *But seek ye first the kingdom of God, and his righteousness; and all these things shall be added unto you.*
>
> *Matthew 6:33*

I was not seeking God first. I was seeking what "I" wanted to happen in my life. I was seeking after the things that "I" wanted. Not concerned with the consequences, I would pay for doing things "my" way. Although I didn't realize it then, all of the things I was doing were so far-fetched and so far-out. How could the little girl brought up in a Baptist church be doing such things? I take full responsibility for my actions. Although I was being whipped along by forces both inside and outside myself who were demons. I should have known better. These demons were influencing my thoughts, whispering words into my ears, and making me think everything was my own idea.

When Satan comes to you at first, he does not come to you as a lightning bolt. He comes to you as a subtle thought. If your spirit has been damaged through sin, you are separated from God and it is so easy for him to enter your thoughts and make you think you came up with this great idea. The devil and his dark angels will use any and every means to tempt God's people to sin, but God has given us the means to say no to every temptation.

Unfortunately, some of us do not say no. Satan knows two things: Jesus is the true Son of God and hell was created for (Satan) and his fallen angels. The devil and his demons know what the future holds in store for them and they are trying to take as many people with them as possible. If they cannot take you with them, they will tempt you, harass you, and try to neutralize your effectiveness as a Christian. But God has given us the weapons that work against the devil... His Word and the Holy Spirit!

Chapter Six

AFFLICTED WITH SICKNESS

The deceptions of Satan are used in the teachings of the New Age. Prolonged contact with the demonic kingdom results in a transformation of consciousness. The initial experience may appear positive, but afterward there are negative repercussions which include dehabilitation, with-drawal, depression, and destruction.

In the months I spent using creative visualization every night before I went to sleep, I began to experience all of these symptoms. My work production decreased, and my ability to concentrate began to wane. I began to isolate myself from other persons. Rather than increasing the ability to love and reach out to others, I became more self-absorbed, seeking higher spiritual experiences. The highs became fewer while the lows became deeper. The final state of all who surrender to demonic control, under the guise of self-sufficiency, is eternal hell prepared for the devil and his fallen angels.

Each night I would visualize the man I loved leaving his wife. I would even go so far as to visualize the things they would say to each other. I would mentally imprint the image of what I desired upon the causal matrix of the astral world. Then I would give it the force and permanence that would ensure its coming to earthly reality by charging it with the light of my "higher self."

There was great deception in using my imagination, and thinking I was calling upon the power of my "higher self." Actually what I was doing was calling upon the powers of evil spirits to bring about my desires. By projecting a high imagination, I was going against the very Word and knowledge of God. As Paul wrote:

> *For though we walk in the flesh, we do not war after the flesh: (For the weapons of our warfare are not carnal, but mighty through God to the pulling down of strong holds;) Casting down imaginations, and every high thing that exalteth itself against the knowledge of God, and bringing into captivity every thought to the obedience of Christ.*
>
> *II Corinthians 10:3-5*

The deception was in thinking an astral image charged in this way could not fade as a passing thought form might do. The Hindu teaching behind this technique states that in due course, if your work is effectively done, it must come to earthly manifestation. The more resolutely you perform it, the sooner and more completely this will be achieved.

I took very seriously my practice for gaining awareness of and contact with my "higher self." This was a most important step in my creative visualization program, but it was also much more than that. I was putting myself in touch more strongly all the time with my own personal link to what I thought was divine light, energy, and love.

The divine light was supposedly the light within me, a light that had always been there. I must state once again: I was putting faith in *myself*. This was a terrible mistake! No matter how I tried to justify my actions at the time, I was giving Satan power over me.

In creative visualization, you imagine a white light above your head as "your source of power." The light supposedly comes from within you. First you see the light, then you go towards the light, and next you *are* the light. Satan's ultimate lie is that you are capable of being the god of your own life. In meditation and creative visualization, you are calling upon the light of your "higher self," your "higher supreme being with godlike qualities." This is terribly wrong! This is blasphemy towards God! Jesus said:

> *I am the light of the world: he that followeth me shall not walk in darkness, but shall have the light of life.*
>
> *John 8:12*

In case you do not understand this concept of creative visualization, consider this comparison. If you take a photographic negative and draw a shape on it, when the photograph is printed, the shape you have drawn will appear plainly among the objects that were there when the picture was taken. Or to put it another way, if you graft a branch from a peach tree onto an apple tree, at the time for blossoms and for fruit, the branch you have grafted in will produce its own blossoms and fruit just as the rest of the tree will produce its own.

Likewise it is among the shadows of things to come

which exist in the astral world. If you plant the shape of that which you desire and confirm it by charging it with the light of your "higher self" to make sure it lives and prospers, then you know the results will follow in the material world. This is how the deception of using creative visualization would bring that which I desired into earthly reality. In doing this, I was exerting my own, God-given free will in a very manipulative way...by using the forces of evil—a way you usually die from!

After spending nine months with this technique, I reached a point when I started to doubt myself. "Does any of this even work?" I asked myself. I was in such a hurry for Alec and his wife to separate and divorce because I knew that soon they were planning to build a million-dollar home.

Shortly after my twenty-ninth birthday, I became very sick. It was on Friday, October 15, 1993. I felt a piercing pain in the middle of my eyes, the exact place I would call the center eye, which is the evil eye, and in the exact same spot I used in creative visualization with my charging techniques. I felt a sudden, sharp, cutting pain that remained constant. It was different from a headache, much more painful and intense. My body started aching all over as if I had the flu, but they were aches I had never felt before. My fever spiked to 104 degrees. When I took aspirin, my temperature would break slightly and then shoot right back up.

On Wednesday, October 20, 1993, I went to the doctor. I was so weak from vomiting for six days straight that I could barely drive myself to the doctor's office. At this particular time in my life, I was also having problems with my finances and had hardly enough money to pay for a doctor's visit. When I saw the doctor, he told me I had the flu that was going around and said it was nothing for me to worry about. He gave me a shot, prescribed some medicine for me to take, and sent me on my way.

I remember thinking, "Surely he must be wrong. There is no way this could be the flu." I had had the flu before and it had never made me feel like this. I truly felt as though my body was dying. I had no strength. I was scared, not knowing what was wrong with me.

I had always been healthy and fit, always taking vitamins, working out, and keeping my body in shape, but now something was terribly wrong with me. I knew I was about to die from something, but I just did not know what it could possibly be.

When I went to the pharmacy to get my prescription filled, I could barely hold myself up. I was so weak and I knew I was experiencing some sort of sickness I had never encountered before. The color of my vomit, the bile coming out of the pit of my stomach, indicated to me this was no ordinary sickness. It was as though the insides of my flesh were literally rotting from within, and all of the refuse was making its way out of my body through my mouth. I was so sick spiritually, my body was truly dying!

My mother called me that Wednesday night from her home. Isn't it amazing that the love of a mother for her child is so great she can sense when her child is in danger? She called me around 9:00 p.m. and my voice was so weak you could hear death in it. I told her I had been sick for six days with a fever that was now 105 degrees and would not break. I remember saying, "Mother, I think I am going to die! Am I going to die, Mother?" I was right. I was dying; I was physically dying!

My dear, sweet mother, glory be to God Most High for her, she broke out in prayer for me. I can remember that sweet prayer she prayed for me as if it were yesterday. She cried, "Oh, dear Lord, my Father in heaven, this is my first child, Lord. This is my child Laurie, and not only is this my child, Father, but she is your child too, and in the name of Jesus, Father, I ask that this fever be broken and, in the name of Jesus, I *command* that this fever be broken and you keep Laurie safe. Father, I stand on your Word that, if I ask anything in the name of Jesus, my request will be answered, so in the name of Jesus, Father, I make this request of you. Father, I thank you for answering my request. Amen."

As I listened to her every word and prayed with her harder than I have ever prayed for anything in my entire life, I felt the Holy Spirit come in me and break the fever with which Satan had plagued me. In order for Satan and his demons to attack me in full force, I had to become weak—spiritually, mentally, and physically. Though the battle was only halfway over, God had answered my mother's prayer and had broken the terrible fever!

Chapter Seven

TRICKED BY AN ANGEL OF LIGHT

The next day, I was still weak, so very weak you could still hear death in my voice. I remember talking to Anna that Thursday night, "Well, Anna, guess what? My mother broke my fever last night. And you know what else? God doesn't hear my prayers, but He heard my mother's."

Anna, being the skeptical lawyer she is, said, "Okay, Laurie, I am glad your mother prayed for you and broke your fever." Anna was the lawyer I had worked for and was also one of my friends. She surely thought I was out of my mind, but she also knew how sick I had been. Anna had come by to check on me several times and had expressed her concerns.

Though my fever had subsided, I was still very weak and sick. Something was obviously wrong with me. A strange feeling came over me and I knew something had happened. I got myself together as best I could and I drove to the house where Alec and his wife had lived.

OUT OF DARKNESS...INTO THE LIGHT

Six months before, they had moved into a patio home about three blocks away because they were going to tear down the house they had been living in and build a new house on the property. The old house was still sitting empty on the lot.

As I rounded the curve, I gazed through the woods and saw lights on in their old house. There was some activity going on. As I drew closer to the house, I saw a moving truck in the driveway and someone was moving in. I knew they had not sold the house because they were going to tear it down. But here was someone moving into the house.

I drove closer and I knew then; it was Alec. He had separated from his wife and was moving back into his house. My love spell had worked! It was the weirdest feeling I have ever felt. All the time I had practiced my creative visualization had finally paid off; they were separated at last.

I had used creative visualization and mind energies to bring about my heart's desire. Having accomplished my ultimate goal, it was now time for someone to pay the price for this "success." That someone was me.

As I drove home, the first words out of my mouth were, "Oh, my God, what have I done? I did it, I did it, I did it!!!" I said to myself, "Laurie, you did it." I was so excited, about as excited as a sick person could possibly be, but at the same time, I was filled with sadness. I thought to myself, "Is this really what I want? Is it really?" Here it was; I had just spent nine months working for something and it had materialized on this plane. "Now I can have him, have him for myself," and I still was not happy.

My heart was filled with a great sadness as I realized I had harmed someone, not just someone but an entire family. I had grown up in a family that was destroyed by other women, and here I was, the "other" woman. My parents had divorced when I was young and I thought to myself, "How could I be the same type of woman who caused my very own family so much pain?" But I was and I had taken it one step further. I had dabbled with the powers of the occult. And on top of that, I had used these powers for evil means.

It was evil spirits, demons I had sent to him by the thoughts I was thinking to torment and harass him to the point of breaking up his marriage. God is very clear and His commandments are set forth in the Bible: We must not seek to communicate with spirits and with the dead.

Regard not them that have familiar spirits, neither seek after wizards, to be defiled by them: I am the Lord your God.

Leviticus 19:31

God condemns mediums and spiritualists, classifying them as of Satan and in the same wretched class with sorcerers, diviners, and witches:

There shall not be found among you any one that maketh his son or his daughter to pass through the fire, or that useth divination, or an observer of times, or an enchanter, or a witch, Or a charmer, or a consulter with familiar spirits, or a wizard, or a necromancer. For all that do these things are an abomination unto the Lord: and because of these abominations the Lord thy God doth drive them out from before thee.

Deuteronomy 18:10-12

It is for our protection and salvation that the Lord has established these guidelines. He loves us and desires that we consult with Him for He alone has the answers to all our needs.

When I got back to my apartment, it was late, but I called my friend Anna. I did not tell her what I had done, but I rambled on, not really making much sense in anything I was saying. After our conversation, I went into the bathroom to wash my face. When I looked in the mirror, I noticed my skin looked really weird and it was turning a strange color. When I brushed my teeth, my entire mouth started to taste bitter. My teeth turned a greenish yellow color. The phlegm and bile that were starting to come up out of me as I spit into the sink were a color I had never seen before. I knew something was very wrong and something very strange was happening to me.

I lay down in my bed to go to sleep but couldn't, no matter how hard I tried. There was a buzz in the atmosphere with a pitch so intensely high it caused my ears to ring. Because of the confusion in my mind by the inward buzz of persecuting spirits, fresh ground was given to the powers of darkness, which resulted in a deeper possession through the distraction caused by the interference.

I was exhausted and still so very weak, yet I could not fall asleep. I lay there for several hours. Finally, I decided to use my creative visualization for relaxation. I closed my eyes and tried to imagine my white light above my head, the light of my "higher self" that I used to shape my future.

The bright light that had previously appeared to me as a soothing, luminous light was now a bright, flaming red light. I thought to myself, "Okay, my white light is now red. Why is this happening? What is going on here? I have always been able to imagine this light as white, and if you have changed to red, then red you will have to be. I have been much too sick for far too long to try and get you back to white."

I lay in my bed trying to visualize with a bright red light above my head. I started to imagine the light starting at the top of my head working its way down through the tips of my toes. As I did this, I felt a powerful surge of energy pass through me. I thought at the time I was in control of my light as I was making my body healthier and leaner. I was absorbing all the fat cells in my buttocks and making it firmer, shapelier, and I could actually feel my buttocks growing tighter and leaner. I thought this was rather strange, but if my buttocks were getting smaller and firmer, then it must be all right.

But all of a sudden, I began seeing horrible scenes of people being mutilated and perverted sexual acts I had never seen or thought of before. It scared me so badly I opened my eyes and there seemed to be hundreds upon hundreds of translucent beings all throughout my apartment. They were ghosts, demons, call them what you will, but they were in my apartment and they were in it with *me!*

I shut my eyes hoping I was imagining things. However, when I opened my eyes again, they were still there, everywhere. It was in the early hours of the morning and there was enough light in my room so it was not totally dark, but all I could see was my apartment filled with what I thought were at least a thousand ghosts in it with me. I knew without a doubt from divine revelation these were all the evil spirits I had attracted towards me the whole time I had practiced my creative visualization. The veil had been lifted from my eyes allowing me to see the spirit world. The realm of supernatural spirits as visible and they were trapped in my apartment with me.

I remember the one which scared me the most. He was dressed in a white-and-black-striped shirt and he kept leaning toward me making gestures with his tongue. It was horrifying beyond what your mind could ever believe possible. I screamed at the top of my lungs, "Oh, God, God! Where are you?" Little did I know that my comforter could be so far away because of my sin and rebellion.

> *For these things I weep; mine eye, mine eye runneth down with water, because the comforter that should relieve my soul is far from me...*
>
> *Lamentations 1:16*

I ran into my living room with my Bible, opened it, and started reading in the book of *John, chapter 4:16-36*. This section talks about a woman who is thirsty for water, the water of everlasting life.

> *Jesus saith unto her, Go call thy husband, and come hither. The woman answered and said, I have no husband. Jesus said unto her, Thou hast well said, I have no husband: For thou hast had five husbands; and he whom thou now hast is not thy husband: in that saidst thou truly.*
>
> *John 4:16-18*

> *Jesus said unto her, Woman, believe me, the hour cometh, when ye shall neither in this mountain, nor yet at Jerusalem, worship the*

TRICKED BY AN ANGEL OF LIGHT

Father. Ye worship ye know not what...

John 4:21-22

But the hour cometh, and now is, when the true worshippers shall worship the Father in spirit and in truth: for the Father seeketh such to worship him.

God is a Spirit: and they that worship him must worship him in spirit and in truth.

John 4:23-24

God gave me these Scriptures because they pertained to my situation. The man I was in love with was not my husband, and I had had four other lovers prior to this one who were married and not my husband. And the things I had been worshiping, I knew not what! God is a Spirit, and those who worship Him, must worship Him in spirit and in truth.

I fell down on my hands and knees on my living room floor repenting for what I had done. Even though I had repented, God was not through allowing me to learn the most valuable lesson of my entire life. I wept, "Oh God, God! Where are you?"

Then, all of a sudden, I heard this nice, quiet, soothing voice coming out of my stereo speaker (which was completely turned off) saying, "I am the Son of Bethlehem." And it repeated itself once again, "I am the Son of Bethlehem." I could not believe what I had just heard. All the ghosts had vanished! My stereo was off and yet I heard this nice, soothing voice coming to me from the stereo saying, "I am the Son of Bethlehem."

Well, of course, I thought it was Jesus Himself. I

was so excited! I thought Jesus had spoken directly to me and He had stopped the madness and had saved me; better yet, He had given me a second chance to repent and live for Him. Little did I know that I had been greatly deceived. Satan had appeared to me as an angel of light. I had been tricked by the father of lies himself, Satan.

And no marvel; for Satan himself is transformed into an angel of light.

II Corinthians 11:14

The reason the voice came out of the stereo speaker was the music I used to listen to. I had a CD which contained a song called "666 Edit." Demons came into my home through the music I had played.

I stood up in my living room still thinking I had found God and had heard the voice of the Lord. All of a sudden from the same stereo speaker came a white mist-like spray spewing all over me from my head to my toes. For a moment it was like bubbles. This mist-like spray turned my whole body ghostly white. All I could think of at the time was, "Okay, God, if this is a religious experience like Moses on the mountain, then please just don't make my hair turn gray." Looking back, I would have gladly accepted gray hair if only I had known the consequences of what I was about to face.

The next day was Friday and my skin was still white as ivory, ghostly white. I went to dinner with a friend, but I looked like death and felt even worse. I went to the bathroom in the restaurant and immediately noticed my skin was starting to change colors again. It was going back to the dreadful color it was the day before.

Also my teeth were starting to turn back to the greenish yellow color. Frightened by what I had seen in the mirror, I knew I had to return home. I did not know what was happening to me. All I knew was that I did not want to be seen in public.

I got back to my apartment and collapsed. I knew something really terrible was happening even though I still felt I had had some sort of religious experience from God. If it truly was from God, then why was I turning into such a monstrous-looking creature? My skin glistened with the look of death as though I were a rotting corpse. More bile and gall started foaming out of the pit of my stomach and gushed out of my mouth. As I vomited the black sludge of disintegrating internal tissues, I spit in the sink and became nauseous at the sight of what was coming out of me. I thought, "Why is this happening to me?" But I knew; I knew it was happening because of what I had done and because of my rebellion.

Behold, O Lord; for I am in distress: my bowels are troubled; mine heart is turned within me; for I have grievously rebelled: abroad the sword bereaveth, at home there is as death.

Lamentations 1:20

I was there all alone, wanting so much to see someone, but I had to hide myself.

I sat on my living room floor again, grabbing my Bible and reading the same exact Scriptures, only this time I read aloud. It was as though this same bright red light passed right through me. It started at the top of my head and made its way down my neck. The more I read aloud, the more I saw this light dripping down right through me as if, in a sense, I were bleeding. The light got midway down my legs and I could see it through my jeans. It scared me so badly I stopped reading. I wanted to hear that voice again, the voice I thought was the voice of the Lord. I ran over to the stereo speaker and said, "Where are you? Let me hear you once again! Oh, God, God, I am so scared! Please let me hear your soothing voice!" Then, all of a sudden, I heard this soft, quieting music that sang this verse to me:

> *I am the Son of Bethlehem.*
> *I will always love you.*
> *I will never leave you.*
> *I am here for you when you need me*
> *If you will only open your heart to me.*

It sang this verse to me over and over again. I could hear this music everywhere, singing in my apartment to me. One of Satan's strongest demons were outside of my body, working in the areas of my mind, will, and emotions.

This strong demon had been outside of my body for a very long time, and wanted in. This demon wanted in with a vengeance! Satan gets no greater pleasure than making one of God's children stumble and fall. Satan hates God, and he hates everything that belongs to Him. Even though I had wandered away, I felt that I was still a Christian and I belonged to Christ. This was why Satan was playing this song for me...he was trying to trick me into opening myself up totally. Satan's goal was to take full possession of my body and soul or should I say, my mind, will, and emotions.

I walked back to my stereo speaker and was staring into it when, all of a sudden, I saw this little dwarf-like black girl, dressed in a red-and-black-checked top and black, tight-fitting pants. I asked her if she were my guardian angel. She nodded her head, "Yes." She started to dance as though she were rapping to some beat. As she danced, her hands moved very fast up and down, back and forth.

I asked her if God had forgiven me. She nodded her head, "Yes."

I thought, "God is cool!" I said, "What do I need to do? What should I do next?" Then, it suddenly came to me I needed to collect all the books in my apartment that were evil, everything I had purchased in the last year—books, candles, witchcraft paraphernalia, tapes, and books on everything from magic spells and creative visualization to powers of the subconscious mind.

I gathered them all together and asked her what I was to do with them. She nodded her head and I knew I was to burn them. When I asked how, she mentally spoke to me saying, "Just go and I will show you." I carried them outside my apartment complex in the dark of the night, making at least ten trips. When I bent over and struck a match to some of the books, everything went up in flames right before my very eyes with an explosion I could not explain. I pointed my right index finger at the fire, and as the fire burned, everything burning was making a stream of red into the tip of my finger. I stood there amazed for at least a half hour, just watching the flames burning. All of a sudden, a man I had never seen appeared and told me to go back inside. Not knowing what I was about to face, I did as I was told.

When I returned to my apartment, I looked at my stereo speaker and said, "Where are you? My friend, where are you?" Looking back, how could I have been so blind as to think that this little black dwarf was my friend, much less my guardian angel? It was an angel all right, one of Satan's dark angels pretending to be my friend. I called to her again and then, out of nowhere, she appeared. As I stood staring at my stereo speaker, she started dancing again, moving so fast I just stood there in amazement.

I asked her all sorts of questions about myself. I asked her if the man whom I had separated would go back to his wife. She shook her head, "No." It seemed as though this thing, whatever it was, knew a lot about me. She even told me I needed to go to the doctor and get checked out because I had something wrong with me. She said I had "the shrimp." I asked her, "What do you mean I have 'the shrimp'?" She said I was having female problems. Sure enough, later in the year, I underwent surgery for endometriosis. Her conversation was the strangest thing I had ever experienced. She even knew about my drug days and especially my taking Ecstacy. She said, "Girl, that stuff was bad, bad, bad for you!"

Can you imagine something or someone telling you about yourself and all the things you had done during your entire life or from the very first time you ever sinned? My only explanation is that, when you sin, you damage your spirit. Through sin, you have an open door for Satan to attack you. When you do not repent of your sin, you attract and draw Satan's negative energies, which are nothing more than evil spirits, to you. These energies or demons sort of hang out with you and influence your thoughts. They are on your brain, outside your mind, harassing and influencing you constantly.

She started dancing again and then, suddenly, a red mist-like spray spewed out from the speaker, spraying all over me. The energy that zapped me felt very uncomfortable. I asked her what God would have me do next. She said, "Get down in your closet and pray." I took heed to what she said, being more assured that she was my guardian angel. As I knelt down in my closet, I asked her if she were leaving. When she said, "Yes," I asked her if I would ever see her again, and she assured me I would. I tried to pray, but I was more concerned if I would ever see her again. By not wanting her to go, I had opened myself up to her and other evil spirits and, unknowingly, was inviting them inside me. I was so blinded by their deception, I actually gave more and more ground to these evils spirits every time I would communicate with them. Communication of this sort is forbidden by God.

As I tried to pray, hundreds upon hundreds of ghosts appeared again, running around me and into my closet. All of a sudden, words of blasphemy towards God resounded through my apartment. I said, "There is no way you could be from God!"

The ghosts answered, "We know; we are not! We are the hounds of hell and you've been haunted and we are going to haunt you for the rest of your life!!! We are the hounds of hell, Laurie, and you've been haunted and we are going to haunt you for the rest of your entire life. We are never going to get out of you. We do not want to!!!"

These demons were no longer outside me; they felt like they were inside me—not just one, but three demons. They would not stop the vile words of blasphemy cursing God and me. I screamed, "Get out of me! God, get them out of me!"

They replied, "We are never going to leave; we do not want to get out of you, Laurie. You are crazy and even God can't save you now because you are now haunted for the rest of your life. We are here to stay!"

I screamed back, "There is no way I will let you do this to me!" I was horrified and frantic from the things I was hearing. Imagine another person or thing inside you trying to take possession of your soul—your mind, will, and emotions—trying to take control over all your thoughts and your very own body. I was living my own horror story worse than you see in the movies. But it was real and it was happening to me. The demons said, "We have been on your brain all along. We have been outside you all along. And now that you thought we were your friends, we tricked you and you let us in! We are in you, Laurie, and we will not come out of you! We are the hounds of hell and we are going to haunt you for the rest of your life!"

I knew if there was anywhere I could get help, it would be in a godly place. I drove to a local Baptist church where I found three student pastors, and I tried to explain to them what was happening to me. I told them of the New Age activities I was involved in which caused this to happen. But never having been exposed to anything like this, they did not know how to deal with it. Of course, they prayed with me and at that time the demons would shut up. But as soon as the prayer was over, the demons would start speaking again, saying the same horrible things. I was in tears and terrified! I thought, "If these pastors cannot help me, who on earth can?"

The demons kept saying over and over, "Laurie, you are crazy! Look at you, Laurie. Listen to what you are saying. You are crazy! These pastors think you are crazy, too. They are going to send you to the crazy house. Laurie, why don't you just shut up before they take you away!"

The demons tried to control my reflexes in both my arms, making both my arms flap up and down like the wings of a bird. Amazed, the student pastors asked, "What are you doing?"

I said, "I don't know. It is not me doing it. Please, please help me! Would all of you please help me?!" The spiritual torment was pushing my mind and emotions to the edge.

The pastors wanted to call the police and take me to the psychiatric ward at the county hospital. Thank God, I still had some wits about me for I would not let them. I begged and pleaded that they just let me go back home. I told them I would call friends and have them take me somewhere to get help. They almost would not let me leave. One pastor said, "You are in no condition to get in your car and drive anywhere. We are notifying the police."

I said, "Please, I came to you for help. Please do not do this. Please help me!"

They answered, "Ma'am, we have already prayed with you. What more can we do for you? We cannot hear any of the things you are hearing."

I tried to explain I had dabbled in the occult and practiced witchcraft, I had separated a man from his wife by doing a manipulative love spell, and I had been tricked by demons who at first were outside me, then tricked me and were now inside me. I might as well have been speaking in another language since they did not have a single clue about what was happening to me and it was far beyond their realm of understanding. It is really astonishing the number of Christian ministers today who disclaim the reality of evil spirits and that there is a Satan who leads his own force of dark angels. To deny Satan and his demons is to deny the very Word of God. The Bible says Jesus Christ's mission to earth was for the express purpose of destroying the works of the devil:

> *He that committeth sin is of the devil; for the devil sinneth from the beginning. For this purpose the Son of God was manifested, that he might destroy the works of the devil.*
>
> *I John 3:8*

We find clear examples of this work:

> *When the even was come, they brought unto him many that were possessed with devils; and he cast out the spirits with his word, and healed all that were sick.*
>
> *Matthew 8:16*

Why the church in the twentieth century has not recognized the existence, and workings, of evil supernatural forces, can only be attributed to its low condition of spiritual life and power. Even at the present time, when the existence of evil spirits is recognized by the secular world, it is generally looked upon by the majority of the church as "superstition" and ignorance. The ignorance is often on the part of the church, who is blinded by the prince of the power of the air to the revelation given in the Scriptures, concerning the Satanic powers.

The "ignorance" on the part of the secular world is in the propitiatory attitude toward evil spirits. Because of the ignorance of the gospel message of a Deliverer and a Saviour set to "proclaim release to the captives" *(Luke 4:18),* and Who, when He was on earth, went about healing all who were "oppressed by the devil" *(Acts 10:38),* and sent His messengers to open the eyes of the bound ones, that they might "turn from darkness to light, and from the power of Satan unto

God" *(Acts 26:18).*

However, the Holy Spirit is already at work, opening the eyes of the people of God. Many of the leaders in the Church are beginning to recognize the real existence of Satanic powers, and are seeking to know how to discern their workings, and how to deal with them in the power of God.

The pastors allowed me to return to my apartment but still notified the police. The entire time, the demons inside me kept saying, "You are crazy. You are crazy, Laurie. You are going to jail, Laurie. You are going to jail. They think you are crazy, and they are going to take you away."

They must have repeated this a thousand times. I thought to myself, "Why me? What did I do to allow this to happen to me?" But I knew. I had opened the door to Satan and his evil demons by becoming involved with magic and the occult. What I had put out there was now returning to me three-fold.

We know that God tempts no man to sin and yet all are tempted, therefore all are attacked by Satan.

It is easier for Satan to get the victory if you are weak, spiritually, mentally and physically, or all of these as I was. Satan and his demons are the ones who had plagued me with the fever and sickness in order to attack me in full force. All of this happened because I opened myself to the occult, and manipulated the free will of another human being, causing him to separate from his wife.

There is a divinely appointed order in the universe. When it is violated, there's a price to pay, and therefore my sins were returning to me three-fold! I had brought a curse upon myself. You may be asking, "What is a curse?" Well, if you go back to the old covenant of the Bible, you will find:

But it shall come to pass, if thou wilt not hearken unto the voice of the Lord thy God, to observe to do all his commandments and his statutes which I command thee this day; that all these curses shall come upon thee, and overtake thee: Cursed shalt thou be in the city, and cursed shalt thou be in the field. Cursed shall be thy basket and thy store.

Cursed shall be the fruit of thy body, and the fruit of thy land, the increase of thy kine, and the flocks of thy sheep. Cursed shalt thou be when thou comest in, and cursed shalt thou be when thou goest out.

The Lord shall send upon thee cursing, vexation, and rebuke, in all that thou settest thine hand unto for to do, until thou be destroyed, and until thou perish quickly; because of the wickedness of thy doings, whereby thou has forsaken me.

The Lord shall make the pestilence cleave unto thee, until he have consumed thee from off the land, whither thou goest to possess it. The Lord shall smite thee with a consumption, and with a fever, and with an inflammation, and with an extreme burning, and with the sword, and with blasting, and with mildew; and they shall pursue thee until thou perish.

The Lord will smite thee with the botch of Egypt, and with the emerods, and with the scab, and with the itch, whereof thou canst not be healed. The Lord shall smite thee with madness, and blindness, and astonishment of heart.

And thou shalt grope at noonday, as the blind gropeth in darkness, and thou shalt not prosper in thy ways: and thou shalt be only oppressed and spoiled evermore, and no man shall save thee.

The Lord shall smite thee in the knees, and in the legs, with a sore botch that cannot be healed, from the sole of thy foot unto the top of thy head.

If thou wilt not observe to do all the words of this law that are written in this book, that thou mayest fear this glorious and fearful name, THE LORD THY GOD; Then the Lord will make thy plagues wonderful, and the plagues of thy seed, even great plagues, and of long continuance, and sore sicknesses, and of long continuance.

Moreover he will bring upon thee all the diseases of Egypt, which thou wast afraid of; and they shall cleave unto thee.

Also every sickness, and every plague, which is not written in the book of this law, them will the Lord bring upon thee,, until thou be destroyed.

Deuteronomy 28:15-22,27-29,35,58-61

You can see from these Scriptures that sickness is a curse of the Law. Demons are the enforcers of a curse. The dreadful diseases enumerated here—in fact, every sickness and every disease, according to the 61st verse—are part of the punishment for breaking God's law.

The King James Version of these Scriptures would lead us to believe that God himself puts sickness and afflictions upon His people for it reads, "The Lord will smite thee...." Dr. Robert Young, author of *Hints to Bible Interpretation,* points out that, in the original Hebrew, the verb is in the permissive rather than the causative sense. Therefore, it might also be translated something like this: "The Lord will allow you to be smitten. The Lord will allow these plagues to be brought upon you."

So, no, God does not send plagues and sickness upon His people as these verses seem to indicate. God's Word does not teach that these things come directly from God. When God's people broke His commandments, they no longer were under His divine protection. He permitted the devil to bring those afflictions upon them. Sin and wrongdoing brought these dreadful plagues upon them, and upon me! The things I was afflicted with—the burning, blindness, and madness—are referred to in *Deuteronomy 28*, which lists several diseases in the curse of the broken Law. Among them are pestilence, consumption (tuberculosis), fever (including all types such as typhus, scarlet, syphiloid, smallpox, and all other eruptive fevers), inflammation, extreme burning, the botch of Egypt, emerods, scab (all skin diseases), itch, madness, and blindness.

> *Christ hath redeemed us from the curse of the law, being made a curse for us: for it is written, Cursed is every one that hangeth on a tree.*
>
> *Galatians 3:13*

What is the curse of the Law? The only way to find out is to go back to the Law. The expression, "the Law" as found in the New Testament, usually refers to the Pentateuch, the first five books of the Bible. As we go back to these books, or the Law, we find the curse, the punishment for breaking God's Law, is threefold: poverty, sickness, and spiritual death.

These things were happening to me because I had broken God's Law and I was no longer under His divine protection. But at this point, I could not have just said, "Okay, this is what I know, God. I repent. Make it stop." Because of my rebellion, stubbornness, and unforgiveness, I had been delivered to the tormentors.

And his lord was wroth, and delivered him to the tormentors, till he should pay all that was due unto him. So likewise shall my heavenly Father do also unto you, if ye from your hearts forgive not every one his brother their trespasses.

Matthew 18:34-35

While I recognize some who have sinned deeply are delivered very quickly. For many others it is a long and torturous road back from out of the darkness into the light. In my case, the torment would not stop until, with God's help, I had torn down the destructive strongholds and had ripped out the ungodly roots that were controlling my mind and flesh. I had to strengthen my faith by choosing to believe God's word, even when I did not see immediate results, rather than the lies of the enemy. Repeatedly I had to forgive myself and others and expect, by faith, that God had forgiven me. I had to repent of rebellion and stubbornness, and then choose to believe that the Lord had cleansed me from all unrighteousness.

As a Christian, you do not accept Christ and then turn away from Him to explore the "other" side whether it be innocent dabbling or just simply through curiosity. I never *felt* I was worshiping Satan. The whole time I practiced creative visualization, I was putting my faith in my "higher self." I was trusting in myself. This was a tragic mistake! If you are not putting your faith in God, you are putting your faith in something else...and again, that something else is Satan. Whether you do it deliberately or not, the end result is always the same. You leave yourself wide open to Satan and his demons.

Chapter Eight

PROVING MY FAITH IN JESUS

The police came knocking at my door, and they scared me to death. I was still so weak and yet trying to keep some kind of composure. They stayed with me until Anna, my lawyer friend, showed up. I convinced them, as best I could, that I was okay and they finally left. I tried to tell Anna what had been happening and her mind was baffled. Not knowing what else to do, we called my mother. She was in the middle of a tea for my brother's wife-to-be that weekend, so she could not just drop everything and fly to Houston. As I related the events of the last two days, she understood what I poured out to her. At last, someone understood and believed me.

I was having to fight these demons for my very own soul. My mother prayed with me, but this time even her prayers could not break the hold the demons had upon me. They had hold of me firmly and they did not want to let go.

My mother knew of my interest in the New Age Movement. She knew of my interest in meditation and how I was interested in the powers of my mind. She knew and she had warned me many times, "Laurie, the wages of sin is death."

For the wages of sin is death; but the gift of God is eternal life through Jesus Christ our Lord.

Romans 6:23

I wish I had taken heed to what she instructed because she had been right all along. My dear, sweet mother must have placed my name on many prayer lists during this time. I could not even estimate the number of times I called her in the next forty-eight hours. She told my little sister and other members of my family what was happening to me.

My sister spoke with Anna during one of the times we called, asking her questions as to how I looked. Anna told her my face was distorted and I kept sweating profusely. Anna said, "She doesn't even look like the Laurie I know. She is white, ghostly white, and her skin is very cold!"

I spoke with my mother again and she told me, "Laurie, you have to hold on. You must hold on, and only through Jesus Christ our Lord and Saviour will you be able to."

I knew I had been saved many, many years before when at the age of eight I walked down the aisle of First Baptist Church and gave my life to Christ. I knew there was a God and He had sent His only Son into this world to save me from all my sins, and all I had to do was trust and believe in Him. I had accepted this

PROVING MY FAITH IN JESUS

fact such a long time ago, yet the experience I was about to have would be the greatest test of my faith.

My mother gathered with a group of ladies including my two aunts to pray fervently for me. Others who prayed for me were my sister and brother and the many people they contacted from different churches. I had well over a thousand people praying for me just in their community.

My mother told my sister, "Rebecca, this is very serious! This is a life-and-death situation! We cannot reach Laurie fast enough to help her! Rebecca, we must pray! Contact as many people as you can and tell them what is happening to Laurie and ask them to start praying for her immediately! Ask them to pray fervently! Pray and fast without ceasing!" It was the prayers of my loved ones which saved me. They stood in the gap for me and interceded.

The prayer they prayed for me was an intercessory prayer of exorcism on my behalf. The powers that bound me were headquartered in the heavenlies where "the prince of the power of the air" is enthroned, but Jesus has given His church the power to bind Satan.

> *Upon this rock I will build my church; and the gates of hell shall not prevail against it. And I will give unto thee the keys of the kingdom of heaven: and whatsoever thou shalt bind on earth shall be bound in heaven: and whatsoever thou shalt loose on earth shall be loosed in heaven.*
>
> *Matthew 16:18-19*

The goal for intercessory prayer was to release my will in order for me to respond directly to the Lord and receive help from God. Since I had been bound by the bondage of sin and of Satan by decisions of my own free will, binding the devil would not cause me to turn. However, when the demonic powers were bound by the prayers of my mother, two aunts, family, and others, I then had the ability to choose Christ and His kingdom.

The prayer for relieving such bondage must involve the exercise of consummate faith in Jesus and spiritual maturity reflected in prayer and fasting. The power of the blood of Jesus must be called upon to "cover" the victims of such demonic activity. It was their prayers for me that would save me, and an act of faith in God on my part that would deliver me.

Other times I called my mother screaming, "Mother, please help me! Make it stop!"

She would answer, "Laurie, we have prayed for you, but it is you who have to do it. You must have faith and fight Satan and his demons. Laurie, you are fighting for your life, soul, and salvation. Keep repeating, 'Jesus is in me. Christ lives and died for me. I belong to Jesus and I am a child of the King.' For God's Word says, 'Greater is He that is in you than he that is in the world.' There is great power in the name of Jesus. He will surround you with angels and keep you safe. Do not fear. Fear is of the devil. Do not stop for a single second."

The Bible says:

> *For by grace are ye saved through faith; and that not of yourselves: it is the gift of God.*
>
> *Ephesians 2:8*

My mother spoke to Anna again and told her I had to keep repeating "Jesus is in me" to build up my faith.

I kept repeating over and over what my mother had said for me to repeat, "Jesus is in me, Jesus is in me."

Mother said, "Laurie, this is what you have to do and you must believe it with all your heart and soul. Keep saying it. Say it over and over. Do not stop for a single minute." And that is what I did. I repeated continuously every single second for the next forty-eight hours, "Jesus is in me, Jesus is in me."

My goodness, how I must have scared my mother with this experience! She could not drop everything and come to me and, even if she could, I think the Lord told her to stay for she knew what I had done and she knew that God was about to deal with me and teach me the most valuable lesson of my life.

Anna called another friend, Tim (not his real name), who was very close to me. Anna and Tim never left my side for the next three days and I thank God for them. They took me to several churches and told people what had happened to me. Each time, I was prayed over, anointed, or blessed with holy water. The pastors laid their hands on me, but nothing, it seemed, could break the grip of Satan and his demons.

Even the pastors didn't understand what was happening to me. They told Anna and Tim I was not possessed by demons. If I were, they said, the demons would have left when they prayed over me and laid their hands upon me. But there is an example in the Bible when even Jesus' disciples could not cast a demon out of a person. When they asked Jesus why they could not:

And he said unto them, This kind can come forth by nothing, but by prayer and fasting.

Mark 9:29

I have to identify myself with this example in the Bible and take the example even one step further... only my faith could save me now. Still, the whole time I kept repeating, "Jesus is in me, Jesus is in me, Jesus is my Saviour, Christ died for me."

It was late into the night. Anna and Tim thought if only I would go to sleep and get some rest, the madness would stop, but instead the demons kept screaming and repeating words of blasphemy over and over. This is what mental torture is like. Including psychological warfare with induced sleep depravation. There was no way I could sleep with the horrible noises in my head.

The demons kept telling me if I went to sleep, I would die and they would take me to hell with them. They told me over and over: "We are taking you to hell when you go to sleep. We are taking you to hell, Laurie. Don't go to sleep because we are taking you to hell when you do!" I couldn't even count all the lies the demons told me. The demons were lying to me to such an extent I was being brainwashed.

Brainwashing is telling someone a lie over and over until the lie is believed. Once the lie is believed, a person loses all sense of self, all sense of his identity. The demons were stripping my mind of everything I had ever known.

Anna and Tim took me to Anna's apartment after we had come from having people pray over me. They just could not believe that something was in me, that I had been invaded by demons, because they could not hear them. But I could hear them and the torment, the mental torment with which these demons were afflicting me! They would not stop what they were saying. They just kept repeating themselves over and over and over again. All I could do was keep repeating, "Jesus is in me, Jesus is in me, Jesus is my Saviour, Jesus is in me."

The minute we walked into Anna's apartment, her two cats went crazy. Animals can tell when demons are present. They were running around like wild animals and this is when Anna and Tim could finally sense some truth to what I was saying. Still, their minds could not even begin to understand what I was going through and what was happening to me.

From Anna's apartment, we went to the emergency room at the hospital. Tim thought maybe if they gave me something to make me sleep, the madness would stop. Of course, the doctor in the emergency room ran all sorts of tests. He tested me for drugs first and could not find any in my system. I had already told him he would not find any. By this time, I had been taken over by spirits to such a state my eyes were glazed and my pupils were huge. It was at this point things began to get worse. The object of Satan's plan for me was to leave me stripped of everything... everything I had ever known.

My life, as I had previously known it, was over, or so these demons wanted me to believe. They continued with their torment saying, "We are going to make you fall in love with us; you belong to us now." It is hard to explain the torture, the madness, Satan and his demons were inflicting upon me.

I wanted to call my mother again. I had already made several calls to her that day. The demons told me if I tried to call my mother one more time, I was going to meet Satan and hear his voice. The demons did not want me talking with my mother since she was the only person who believed what I said and what was actually happening to me. She would reinforce what I needed to keep repeating, "Jesus is in me, Jesus is in me, Jesus is my Saviour, Christ died for me."

I called one last time, and the voices did change. Although the demons were still there, he was now there too—Satan, "the power of the air." The voices did not change until the very end because Satan cannot be everywhere at the same time. Only God can be since He is omnipresent. Because Satan is not omnipresent, he uses his evil demon spirits to do his will for him and to spread his evil spirit until it is time for him to intervene with even more torment.

He spoke to me as I dialed my mother's telephone number. He said, "Laurie, I am in you. I am in you, Laurie. Can you feel me in you?" His voice was so eerie sounding, like none I have ever heard. I could feel him in me gripping and squeezing my very soul. The fits of horror and terror he struck in me were indescribable. He warned me that, if I called my mother, he would get in her too. Oh, how this scared me. As she answered the phone, I cried out, "Mother!" Yet she could hardly tell it was me. "Laurie, is that you?" she asked.

"Mother, please help me! He is in me!"

She replied, "Laurie, I cannot understand a word you are saying."

I pleaded, "Mother, please help me! He is in me!" But she still could not understand a single word I said.

As I tried to speak, Satan distorted every word I would say. I felt the words bouncing back at me from the telephone receiver. I cried out again, "Mother, please help me! He is in me! Please help me, Mother! I can feel him in me! Please help me, Mother! He is in me, and he is gripping and squeezing my soul. Please help me, Mother! He is in me!" I was severely oppressed and had no comforter, and my oppressor had great power. All of a sudden, the phone went dead.

PROVING MY FAITH IN JESUS

SO I returned, and considered all the oppressions that are done under the sun: and behold the tears of such as were oppressed, and they had no comforter; and on the side of their oppressors there was power, but they had no comforter.

Ecclesiastes 4:1

I hung up the phone and my friends took me back to the examining room. When the doctor returned, Satan told me the doctor was going to do terrible things to me. As the doctor strapped the EKG machine to me, the machine was going crazy. I had so much demonic energy inside of me, my entire body was about to explode. The Ebola virus pales in comparison to what I encountered.

Satan even tried to speak through me to the doctor, but I would not let him. I kept fighting him. I could feel the words trying to come out of my mouth, but I continued to say silently, "Jesus is in me, Jesus is in me, Jesus is my Saviour, Christ died for me." I concentrated on saying this the entire time. From the very first time I spoke with my mother and she told me I would have to fight for my very own soul, I fought him. I fought him for my life! I knew that if I gave up and allowed his voice to speak through me, he would have more control.

Satan kept saying, "I am in you, Laurie. Give up! You belong to me now! Can you feel me in you? I am in you, Laurie! Give up! Give up! You are mine!"

Over and over, I never stopped, not even for a single moment, the entire time. I just kept repeating, "Jesus is in me, Jesus is in me, Jesus is my Saviour, Christ died for me." The nurse came in with some pills for me to take, but I refused to take them because Satan and his demons kept telling me that, once I fell asleep, they were taking me with them to hell. They said, "Laurie, when you take those pills, you are going to die. You are going to go to sleep and die. Laurie, we are taking you to hell with us when you do!" The demonic oppression was making me mad.

Surely oppression maketh a wise man mad...

Ecclesiastes 7:7

I cannot describe the intensifying terror that surged deep within me, even unto my very soul! I felt the anger and rage of this beast inside me and my heart pounded harder with every beat. I just knew that any minute it would explode right out of my chest and blood would spew everywhere. My insides felt like they were being turned inside out.

O Lord, behold my affliction: for the enemy hath magnified himself.

Lamentations 1:9

There were two opposing forces fighting a war inside me—a force who wanted me to die, and a force who wanted me to live!

I remember looking at Anna and crying, "There is no way I can live like this for the rest of my life! There is no way! My body is about to explode!" But something in me still kept repeating, "Jesus is in me, Jesus is in me, Jesus is my Saviour, Christ died for me."

Satan had even reversed the roles of my two caring friends. He kept telling me, "Those are not your friends,

PROVING MY FAITH IN JESUS

Laurie. Those are not your friends. We are your only friends now. We will make you fall in love with us; just watch...."

Tim and Anna knew I had no hospital insurance at the time. Tim had previously told me he would pay for everything if I had to stay. All of a sudden, Tim said, "Laurie, write them a check so we can hurry up and go home."

I said, "What? I thought you were going to pay for it."

He said, "Laurie, write the check. Who cares if it bounces? You are not ever getting out of here anyway, so go ahead and write these people a check."

Anna said, "Hurry up, Laurie. Write the check. We are tired and ready to go home. Write the check, Laurie."

I said, "My car, what about my car?" At the time, I had a beautiful sports car.

They said, "Don't worry about your car, Laurie. We will keep your car and sell it."

I said, "My apartment, my home, all of my things...."

They said, "Laurie, your family will be here tomorrow and they will do something with your apartment and things."

I could not believe my ears. These two people, these two caring friends of mine...how could Satan have influenced their thoughts and reversed their roles? But he did. It was only temporary, of course, and only at this particular instance did he reverse their roles. My only explanation for this is that he was right there near them, able to influence their way of thinking.

My friends had decided to admit me and were going to leave me in the hospital for observation. They came into the room and urged me to take the pills. Having no other choice except to take them, I agreed only if they would let me go into the chapel at the hospital and pray one last time...one last time before I died! The whole time I knew I was about to die, but I still kept the faith. I kept saying, "Jesus is in me, Jesus is in me, Jesus is my Saviour, Christ died for me."

I finally took the pills. As they walked me back into the pavilion area where I was to stay, they let me go into the chapel and pray. I wanted to pray for my soul one last time before I died. I knelt down and looked at the Bible and words started to disappear off the page they were written on. Satan even tried to delete from my memory every Scripture I had ever learned.

> *And that from a child thou hast known the holy scriptures, which are able to make thee wise unto salvation through faith which is in Christ Jesus.*
>
> *II Timothy 3:15*

Satan even tried to delete my most favorite verse:

> *For God so loved the world, that he gave his only begotten Son, that whosoever believeth in him should not perish, but have everlasting life.*
>
> *John 3:16*

I would say, "For God so loved the world...," and my mind would go blank. Satan and his demons laughed, "You can't even say it, can you? Say it, Laurie. Let us hear you say it."

With waning strength, I would then attempt to say it again, "For..." and I could not remember one more word of my most favorite Scripture. Satan brought in such confusion that everything of God seemed so far from me.

He said: "Even God cannot save you now. You are mine, Laurie. I will make you fall in love with me, Laurie. You belong to me now. Give up!"

Words continued to disappear off the pages of the Bible as I knelt to pray. I cried, "Oh, dear God. This is Laurie, and I am your child. I have always been your child, Lord, since the day I chose Jesus as my Saviour. I know I have done wrong by straddling the fence between good and evil. And I may have strayed too far. But if you will please save my soul and get me out of this mess I have gotten myself into, I won't care if I have to fight these demons every day for the rest of my life. I claim Jesus Christ as my Lord and Saviour and I will not forsake Him. If it is your will for me to die this very minute, I will die for Christ's name sake!"

As I tried to pray, I felt my words literally bouncing back at me from heaven. It was as if there were a barrier between me and heaven.

Also when I cry and shout, he shutteth out my prayer.

Lamentations 3:8

As I continued to pray, my words bounced back at me as if there were no hope for my salvation. The shock of panic, horror, and desperation I felt when I was trying to pray for God to save my soul and my prayers were bouncing back at me from heaven. I was surrounded by the powers of darkness and I had been placed into the hands of the devil. Satan and his demons laughed and mocked me as I would attempt to pray for my soul. Satan and his demons viciously taunted me as they tried to break my spirit by sinking me deeper into the dungeon of doubt and despair.

This is what it will be like during the great tribulation period. The world will experience the powers of darkness in such a way it has never encountered in all the history of time.

The powers of darkness were so thick that I could not feel any spirit of prayer. The powers of darkness were pressing so, I could not put words together to form a prayer.

> *Thou hast covered thyself with a cloud, that our prayer should not pass through.*
>
> *Lamentations 3:44*

I had been placed into the hands of the devil.

> *The yoke of my transgressions is bound by his hand: they are wreathed, and come up upon my neck: he hath made my strength to fall, the Lord hath delivered me into their hands, from whom I am not able to rise up.*
>
> *Lamentations 1:14*

I continued to pray for myself harder than I have ever prayed for anything. I pushed those words out of my mouth trying to penetrate the blockade between me and God. The hour of need always brings the corresponding measure of power from God to meet that need. In the end, demons are no match for a sincere person who repents and calls upon the name of the Lord, Jesus!

Submit yourselves therefore to God. Resist the devil, and he will flee from you.

James 4:7

It is quite sobering to realize just how close I was to spending eternity in hell because I had received the knowledge of the truth and accepted Jesus as my Saviour when I was little. However, if I had not sincerely repented for the way I had been living, I would have been left to suffer the consequences of leading a sinful life.

For if we sin willfully after that we have received the knowledge of the truth, there remaineth no more sacrifice for sins, But a certain fearful looking for a judgment and fiery indignation, which shall devour the adversaries.

He that despised Moses' law died without mercy under two or three witnesses: Of how much sorer punishment, suppose ye, shall he be thought worthy, who hath trodden under foot the Son of God, and hath counted the blood of the covenant,wherewith he was sanctified, an unholy thing, and hath done despite unto the Spirit of grace?

For we know him that hath said, Vengeance belongeth unto me, I will recompense, saith the Lord. And again, The Lord shall judge his people. It is a fearful thing to fall into the hands of the living God.

Hebrews 10:26-31

As I walked out of the chapel, my tongue was set on fire of hell.

And the tongue is a fire, a world of iniquity: so is the tongue among our members, that it defileth the whole body, and setteth on fire the course of nature; and it is set on fire of hell.

James 3:6

A few moments later after my friends departed, I felt my skin burning from the heat. Fire was sent into my bones and it prevailed against me. The fury of hell's fire consumed me. The taste in my mouth was bitter and I was so thirsty.

He hath filled me with bitterness, he hath made me drunken with wormwood.

Lamentations 3:15

I could feel myself burning up as if I were in the midst of flames. My soul was removed far from peace. The sorrows of hell compassed me about, the snares of death prevented me. I wanted so much to have a drink of water to cool my tongue from the heat. I was so thirsty!

When I found a water fountain outside the chapel, I pressed the button and watched as the water came up but disappeared before my very eyes into thin air.

I pressed the button again and watched the water come up only to disappear once again into thin air. I was so thirsty; my tongue and body were burning and I could not get relief!

> *Even so the tongue is a little member, and boasteth great things. Behold, how great a matter a little fire kindleth! And the tongue is a fire, a world of iniquity: so is the tongue among our members, that it defileth the whole body, and setteth on fire the course of nature; and it is set on fire of hell. Therewith bless we God, even the Father; and therewith curse we men, which are made after the similitude of God. Out of the same mouth proceedeth blessing and cursing. My brethren, these things ought not so to be.*
>
> *James 3:5-6, 9-10*

Suddenly, my mouth felt as though it were full of alum and I could no longer speak, not one word. I no longer had a tongue and I felt as though it had been ripped out of my mouth.

> *...the perverse tongue will be cut out.*
>
> *Proverbs 10:31*

I knew at this moment I truly was in hell! My soul was full of troubles. I was counted with them that go down into the pit. A woman with no strength, free among the dead, like the slain that live in the graves, whom the Lord remembers no more. I was cut off from His Hand and I was laid in the lowest pit, in total darkness. There was no peace from the mental torture of Satan and his demons. There was no rest from my affliction. I had been cast into outer darkness to experience the utter horror of this underground abode of evil. Its most dread reality is that those who are cast there are without the hope of communication with God. I was in hell!!!

The gatekeeper walked towards me with chains in his hands and said, "You have been deceived! The whole time you trusted in yourself by putting your faith in something else, you were trusting in Satan as your lord. The sentence of death is in yourself, Laurie! We have tricked you. We have deceived you, and you will spend eternity here in hell!"

> *But we had the sentence of death in ourselves, that we should not trust in ourselves, but in God which raiseth the dead.*
>
> *II Corinthians 1:9*

The gatekeeper chained me to a wall in a dark pit where I was totally isolated from the world.

> *He hath set me in dark places, as they that be dead of old. He hath hedged me about, that I cannot get out: he hath made my chain heavy.*
>
> *Lamentations 3:6-7*

I heard weeping, moaning, and gnashing of teeth. I was instructed to lie down because I was not going anywhere and I would be there for a very long time. The gatekeeper kept saying, "Lie down and be quiet!"

I had been cast into outer darkness and there was no peace from hearing the torturous words of Satan and his demons. I heard them laughing, saying, "Laurie, we are in you and you are in hell! You will burn with us in hell! Your life is over! God cannot save you now. You belong to Satan. You are mine, Laurie, and you are going to burn with me in hell!"

Words cannot describe the remorse I felt. All of my sins and follies passed before me. The grief of this you cannot understand until you have experienced it. At this very moment I felt such darkness and bitterness engulf me.

> *Remembering mine affliction and my misery, the wormwood and the gall. My soul hath them still in remembrance, and is humbled in me.*
>
> *Lamentations 3:19-20*

I saw my life completely reviewed in only a moment of time. Oh, the remorse and sadness I felt!

All I could think of was all of the things I would do differently, if only I could have a second chance. In this state of desolation and isolation I could only think, "If only I had known how horrible this place is! How I wasted my life!" I felt as though I were in the deepest dungeon of Hell!

> *I called upon thy name, O Lord, out of the low dungeon.*
>
> *Lamentations 3:55*

I was there wishing I could escape some of the pain, but with no mouth to cry out words of sorrow to my God. Expecting to die, I closed my eyes and one last time I saw total darkness and I silently said for the last time of my life, "Jesus is in me, Jesus is with me, Jesus is my Saviour, Christ died for me. God, please hear my cry for help and do not leave me in this dreadful place of torment!"

OUT OF DARKNESS...INTO THE LIGHT

O Lord my God, I cried unto thee, and thou hast healed me. O Lord, thou hast brought up my soul from the grave: thou hast kept me alive, that I should not go down to the pit.

Psalms 30:2-3

    I could hear the beating of my heart as it slowed down. I felt it beat until it slowly came to a stop. My heart had stopped beating. I was gasping for air trying to hold onto one last breath of life, but I knew I had ventured into death. I felt trapped in a vacuum to experience the absence of something, the absence of my life. There was no life in my body for I was dead! I was devoid of all life! I remained in this state of emptiness for what seemed like eternity.

    Suddenly I felt myself being carried through a long, dark tunnel; something was carrying me, moving my body so fast with great momentum! I was going toward a bright light at the end of the tunnel. I was moving so swiftly! The next thing I knew, I went through the light! My body was propelled straight up towards the ceiling out of my hospital bed, and I landed to my feet! I awoke screaming at the top of my lungs, "Christ lives, He's alive, He rose from the dead, and He lives; He lives in me! Christ lives, He's alive, and He lives in me!"

    My eyes were wide open, but I could not see; I had been blinded. I could see only a glimmer of light. I didn't care. So excited to be alive, I again shouted with my weakened voice, "Christ lives, He's alive, and He lives in me!" Joy overflowed in my heart. All I could do was rejoice in attempting to shout, "Christ lives, He's alive, He rose from the dead, and He lives; He lives in me!"

I blindly felt my way to the sink, so thirsty for the ever-flowing waters of eternal life. I poured a glass of water and drank deeply. I then poured more water on the top of my head delighting in the cool refreshing waters. I had no control over anything I was doing. It was my spirit that awoke me shouting, "Christ lives," that caused me to pour water on my head as a symbol of being born again. Water is symbolic of the Holy Spirit.

...Except a man be born of water and of the Spirit, he cannot enter into the kingdom of God.

John 3:5

As Charles Kraft points out in his book, *Defeating Dark Angels,* a demon can never completely control a Christian because it cannot live where Jesus is in the person's spirit.

The demons came and held me down, trying to shut me up so I could not scream, "Christ lives!" When I had wakened screaming, "Christ lives," the demons who were in me were expelled. They did not give up so easily though. As they held me down, trying to shut me up, I saw for the first time the one who called himself Satan. He looked like an ox (or bull) with wings. With cloven hooves and horns. Almost the color of a pale pink serpent having a monstrous head with two huge horns. He truly is a beast—an evil beast full of destruction and the world's abominations. He is more horrid-looking than anything in this world that has ever been drawn to depict his likeness. Having four faces, Satan has the face of a man, and yet Satan also resembles what is referred to as an alien. Satan is liken unto cattle and in his natural state, he is a winged bull. Satan is the beast of all beasts! His mission is to deceive you, to trick you, and to rip you apart from the very threads that hold you together.

I looked and saw him for the first time. As I felt his spirit trying to make his way back inside me, I could feel him passing through me, splitting me apart, every cell in my body, and it burned like nothing your mind could ever imagine.

I felt all the hate and anger of this fierce ungodly beast at this one moment in time. The sounds this beast made were sounds I have never heard before. I cannot adequately describe them for they were beyond your realm of comprehension, and for this you must thank God! I felt his spirit trying to pass through me at this very moment with such momentum, trying to rip and split me apart! It felt like the tentacles of a wild animal inside me, squeezing my heart trying to rupture it.

There are no words to describe the torture that will come upon you if you meet up with this roaring lion.

Be sober, be vigilant; because your adversary the devil, as a roaring lion, walketh about, seeking whom he may devour.

I Peter 5:8

I can only pray that no one will ever meet him as I did. And the entire time I kept shouting, "Christ lives, He's alive, and He lives in me!" Praise God, I never lost my faith, not for one second.

The next time I awoke shouting the same words I had shouted before, "Christ lives!" This time the demons tried to give me the mark of the beast on my forehead. They were holding me down trying to make me take it.

Here is wisdom. Let him that hath

> *understanding count the number of the beast:*
> *for it is the number of a man; and his number*
> *is Six hundred threescore and six.*
>
> *Revelation 13:18*

I refused to take it! I fought back with God's Word and my testimony of faith, shouting, "Christ lives, He is alive, He rose from the dead, and He died for me. Christ lives, Christ lives, He lives in me!"

The interpretation of this vision is when people take this mark, they are going to willingly know that they have rejected God and His provisions for salvation through His son, Jesus Christ. Once this mark is taken on the hand or on the forehead, it will be the mark of doom. By taking this mark, a person will never be able to get right with God. They will have sold their soul and become like a demon from hell.

I had a vision of my being confined with huge bugs swarming at me with tails of scorpions, but they could not harm me because I had the seal of God.

> *And he opened the bottomless pit; and there*
> *arose a smoke out of the pit, as the smoke of a*
> *great furnace; and the sun and the air were*
> *darkened by reason of the smoke of the pit. And*
> *there came out of the smoke locusts upon the*
> *earth: and unto them was given power, as the*
> *scorpions of the earth have power. And it was*
> *commanded them that they should not hurt the*
> *grass of the earth, neither any green thing,*
> *neither any tree; but only those men which have*
> *not the seal of God in their foreheads. And to*
> *them it was given that they should not kill them,*
> *but that they should be tormented five months:*

and their torment was as the torment of a scorpion, when he striketh a man. And in those days shall men seek death, and shall not find it; and shall desire to die, and death shall flee from them.

Revelation 9:2-6

The interpretation of this vision is Satan will loose a flood of demon power on earth that has never been experienced in all history. This will be a prelude to worldwide commotion prior to the Great Tribulation itself during the last three and one-half years of Daniel's seventieth week. During this time God is going to allow all the wicked people of the earth who have rejected Him, to experience for five months what hell will be like for all eternity.

The wicked shall be turned into hell, and all the nations that forget God.

Psalms 9:17

What I encountered for three days is what people are going to experience for five months straight. Demonic possession is going to be out of control. These demons are going to torment men the same way they tormented me. Men are going to try to jump out of windows in buildings. Men are going to try to kill themselves any way possible and death is going to flee from them.

I can remember from my experience just wanting the madness to stop and it wouldn't. I cannot even possibly impart the magnitude of what the horror of this experience will be like for people who have to endure this type of judgment for five months straight. God allowed me to experience for three days what hell will be like for all eternity. You see, in hell, people can never die. They will beg to die to escape the torment. They will scream for death, but death will evade them forever.

The saddest part that just breaks my heart is this:

> *And the rest of the men which were not killed by the plagues yet repented not of the works of their hands, that they should not worship devils, and idols of gold, and silver and brass, and stone, and of wood: which neither can see, nor hear, nor walk:*
>
> *Neither repented they of their murders, nor of their sorceries, nor of their fornication, nor of their thefts.*
>
> *Revelation 9:20-21*

It is so easy to turn to God and repent now! Still blinded, I awoke screaming, "Christ lives, He's alive, and He lives in me!"

I had several other visions after this. One was of ugly creatures riding a merry-go-round, slapping me in the face as hard as they could each time they passed me. I suppose this was my spanking from God. Each time I awoke, I could see a little bit more, but not much, just a glimmer of light. Though I was still blind, each time I awoke I was still screaming, "Christ lives, He's alive, and He lives in me. He arose from the dead and He died for me. Christ lives and He lives in me!"

You are probably wondering how God could allow or permit this to happen to me. But I knew the reason.

Each time I awoke, God gave me a vision pertaining to the last days. My entire near death experience was a glimpse into the future, into future things to come. God had blinded me so I could see only what He wanted me to see. Everything that happened to me happened for a reason as a test of my faith. God knew I would keep my faith and I loved Him. I knew this in the hospital, just as I know it now...today. I was faithful unto death and God was faithful to me.

> *For whom the Lord loveth he chasteneth, and scourgeth every son whom he receiveth. If ye endure chastening, God dealeth with you as with sons; for what son is he whom the father chasteneth not? But if ye be without chastisement, whereof all are partakers, then are ye bastards, and not sons. Furthermore we have had fathers of our flesh which corrected us, and we gave them reverence: shall we not much rather be in subjection unto the Father of spirits, and live? For they verily for a few days chastened us after their own pleasure; but he for our profit, that we might be partakers of His holiness.*
>
> *Hebrews 12:6-10*

> *And you hath he quickened, who were dead in trespasses and sins; Wherein in time past ye walked according to the course of this world, according to the prince of the power of the air, the spirit that now worketh in the children of disobedience: Among whom also we all had our conversation in times past in the lusts of our flesh, fulfilling the desires of the flesh and of the mind; and were by nature the children of wrath, even as others. But God, who is rich in*

mercy, for his great love wherewith he loved us. Even when we were dead in sins, hath quickened us together with Christ, (by grace ye are saved).

Ephesians 2:1-5

As many as I love, I rebuke and chasten: be zealous therefore, and repent.

Revelation 3:19

My last vision was of the wings of an Eagle. I could feel the lightness of the wings as they swept across my face. I could feel their soothing lightness as they brushed across my eyes to heal and restore my sight.

But unto you that fear my name shall the Sun of righteousness arise with healing in his wings...

Malachi 4:2

The wings of an Eagle were carrying me away into safety.

He shall cover thee with his feathers, and under his wings shalt thou trust: his truth shall be thy shield and buckler.

Psalms 91:4

The wings of an Eagle are symbolic of supernatural, Divine transport. Swiftness of flight, Divine defense and protection. I could feel the lightness in my heart, the lightness of their wings upholding me.

OUT OF DARKNESS...INTO THE LIGHT

> *And to the woman were given two wings of a great eagle, that she might fly into the wilderness, into her place, where she is nourished for a time, and times, and half a time from the face of the serpent.*
>
> *Revelation 12:14*

I knew I had been carried to a place of safety, rest, and peace. I knew I had been saved! By grace you are saved!!

The next day the doctor came in and asked if I knew who I was. I said confidently, "Laurie Wallace." He told me I had been a very sick girl. He said I had pneumonia in the upper right lobe of my lung. Pneumonia is a serious condition which can cause delirium which leads to death and is almost never benign. The doctor in the emergency room had misdiagnosed my condition and given me a drug called Thorazine. The strong dosage might have put me in a coma, considering my weakened physical condition. God was truly with me as this drug had absolutely no negative effect on me whatsoever.

In this acute form the symptoms of demon possession and insanity are almost indistinguishable. The difference lies in the fact that in pure demon possession the mind is not impaired, although it may be passive, or suspended in action, but in insanity the evil spirit takes advantage of a physical condition. "Insane" people are more "sane" than sane people think they are, and there is more truth in what they say than is believed. What they "see" is not always delusion, but the actual doings of evil spirits. It is necessary, therefore, to distinguish between (1) Pure insanity, (2) Pure "possession," (3) Insanity and possession. Before declaring a person insane, from physical and natural causes, the physician should find out if there be any supernatural cause. Insanity may be caused by natural derangement, and by supernatural interferences of evil powers. True insanity can also be the result of possession, and be (humanly) irrecoverable.

As in my case, I had dabbled with the occult and therefore mine was due to the supernatural workings of evil spirits. I knew without a doubt if I had not kept my faith in Jesus and called upon His name, I would have died!

For whosoever shall call upon the name of the Lord shall be saved.

Romans 10:13

It was only because I loved not my life unto death and kept my faith in Jesus as my Saviour that I lived.

He that findeth his life shall lose it: and he that loseth his life for my sake shall find it.

Matthew 10:39

I stayed in the hospital four days. On the second day after seeing the doctor, I refused to take any more medicine they tried to give me. I talked with the doctor and he asked what had happened to me. I explained to him that the devil had tried to take me to hell and I had called upon the name of Jesus. It was only this that had saved me. The doctor, having seen what I had been through in the last few days, surprisingly believed my story.

On the third day in the hospital, my appetite was restored; I recovered and rested. On the fourth day I left the hospital with full recollection of everything I had been through. The human spirit is designed by God to pick up things our natural mind cannot perceive. This perception comes by revelation. God, by His Holy Spirit, reveals it to our spirit. I knew by divine revelation God had allowed me to experience a brief moment of hell so I could give the world a testimony of warning. A warning of future things to happen during the Tribulation Period. God took advantage of the cruel actions of Satan and his demons to accomplish His divine purpose through me. Often times God uses the destruction of evil and the workings of Satan, to bring glory and honor to His heavenly kingdom.

Because of my faith and I called upon the name of Jesus, I had been given this one last chance to live instead of having to die!

The Lord hath chastened me sore: but he hath not given me over unto death.

Psalm 118:18

I knew this to be the truth the first day in the hospital, just as I know it to be the truth now. I even knew when I came to in the hospital that I was to write of this experience. God by the Holy Spirit revealed it to me.

Spiritual warfare is hell! To be held spiritually captive within your mind torments the soul and exhausts the body. Hell is the worst prison imaginable, a place of torment and torture without a single moment of peace, a place where one will experience great agony both day and night without ceasing, a place of great thirst where there is no water to drink. God was faithful to me, I kept the faith, and I endured until the very end and this is why my life was saved!

> *But he that shall endure unto the end, the same shall be saved.*
>
> *Matthew 24:13*

A lesson in history should teach us that those Americans who have been prisoners of war, in the hands of godless, atheistic Communists, who believed in the Lord Jesus Christ for their salvation have survived where unbelievers perished. As was provided in the case of Western prisoners of war taken in Korea and brainwashed by the captors, it was only those who had a strong faith in fundamental truths who came through their terrible ordeal comparatively unscathed. We have a wonderful promise in God's Word.

> *"There hath no temptation taken you but such as is common to man: but God is faithful, who will not suffer you to be tempted above that ye are able; but will with the temptation also make a way to escape, that ye may be able to bear it."*
>
> *I Corinthians 10:13*

The things I encountered were a life-and-death struggle to loosen myself from the clutches of Satan and his vicious demons. Demons came into me through the open doors of my mind at an early age during my youth through damaged emotions. As I got older, more demons came into me when I did drugs, and had sex outside marriage. Sin opens the door to demonic influence in one's life. Once I became involved with the occult and put my faith in "something else," I gave the enemy and his minions a tremendous amount of power over me. It was truly a life-and-death struggle to escape their evil grasp. But, by the blood of the Lamb, and by the word of my testimony, with God's help I won and I give Him all the glory!

> *And they overcame him by the blood of the Lamb, and by the word of their testimony; and they loved not their lives unto the death.*
>
> *Revelation 12:11*

Many people do not believe in the invisible realm of the spirit world and the host of dark angels who populate Satan's kingdom, but Scriptures prove we should. Paul wrote:

> *Put on the whole armour of God, that ye may be able to stand against the wiles of the devil. For we wrestle not against flesh and blood, but against principalities, against powers, against the rulers of the darkness of this world, against spiritual wickedness in high places. Wherefore take unto you the whole armour of God, that ye may be able to withstand in the evil day, and having done all, to stand.*
>
> *Ephesians 6:11-13*

Paul knew of the existence of the spirit world, the existence of angels, demons, and Satan. There are two powerful forces at work in this world: the kingdom of God and the kingdom of Satan. These kingdoms are at war with each other. You were not designed to function independent of God nor was your soul designed to function as a master. You will either serve God and

His kingdom or Satan and his kingdom. When you deny *yourself* and repent, you invite God to take the throne of your life, to occupy what is rightfully His, so that you may function as a person who is spiritually alive in Christ. Denying yourself is essential to spiritual freedom. Further, the kingdom of God is assured victory because of Jesus' death and resurrection. Which one will you choose?

> *I am crucified with Christ; nevertheless I live; yet not I, but Christ liveth in me: and the life which I now live in the flesh I live by the faith of the Son of God, who loved me, and gave himself for me.*
>
> *Galatians 2:20*

Chapter Nine

IN CLOSING

It took me a year to become strong enough to talk about what happened. For the first month after my experience, I stayed with Anna because I could not stand to be alone in my apartment after what had happened there. I later moved into a new apartment complex. The next six months I slept with every light on and called my mother often in the middle of the night. I would awake during the night feeling my bed shake and a force holding me down. Since then, I have acquired a strong group of prayer partners who have supported me.

In the first six months out of this experience, it was hard for me to dwell on it because, every time I did, I would start hearing in my mind the horrible things Satan and his demons told me throughout the time I was sick. It would take me right back and I had difficulty determining the difference between the memory of what happened to me and the reality of the present world.

I have seen two doctors who gave me absolutely no insight whatsoever into what happened to me. I persisted in reading my Bible and grew stronger through God's Word to make sense of the whole experience. Imagine a POW (prisoner of war) who has been held captive and tortured for days, months, and even years. When he is rescued, he is brought back into a society or world he used to know, but he is never the same. When he thinks about what happened to him, it takes him back to that same place in his life. The memories are horrible. This present warfare seems really bad, but the warfare Satan and his demons waged against me is inconceivable.

After I left the hospital, my hands shook for a month and I could not even hold a cup of coffee without dropping it. My tongue had whelps on it with raw places from where it had been supernaturally burned and it was swollen for several months. To serve as a permanent reminder that I had literally been to hell, anytime I would think a negative thought the bottoms of my feet would start to burn.

I returned to my job in medical sales shortly after I got out of the hospital. Many times I stood in surgery and heard demonic voices calling me, "Laurie, Laurie, we are over here." I kept hearing their voices whispering my name. As they called me, I felt a surge of energy pass through me. The first few months, it frightened me to death and I began to think it would never stop. Each time I would dwell on the horrible things Satan and his demons would say to me, it would take me right back and I would think it was happening all over again.

For a time, I tried to put it out of my mind. My mother suggested I just try to forget it and not tell anyone of this event because people surely would not understand. I tried to take her advice, but this experience is something I am reminded of every day. I now know what the demons meant when they said I had been haunted and they would haunt me for the rest of my life. There is not a day I do not think about what happened. Many times I called my mother crying in the middle of the night, "Mother, will I ever be normal again? I mean, the old me, before I opened myself up to the spirit world?" But I already know the answer. I cannot ever go back...I can only go forward.

Since October of 1993, I have read many books on spiritual warfare. My favorites are *Pigs in the Parlor* by Frank & Ida Mae Hammond; *The Bondage Breaker* by Neal T. Anderson; and *Defeating Dark Angels, Christianity with With Power, Behind Enemy Lines,* and *Deep Wounds, Deep Healing* by Charles H. Kraft.

During the last year, I visited different churches and told pastors of my experience. They began to press me to speak and counsel with others who may be traveling down the same path I had traveled. In the first six months, I just could not go through the mental torture of thinking about it and dwelling upon it. I was not yet strong enough to tell my story to anyone else.

When I turned thirty years old in October of 1994, exactly one year after my experience, I decided it was time to get it down on paper. I wanted to share the entire true story, not just bits and pieces. You have the right to know that Satan exists and has an enormous stronghold in our world today.

The night I started writing this book, I was again attacked by demons. I would close my eyes to fall asleep and actually see them coming towards me. I would rebuke them in the name of Jesus, get my Bible, and start reading. This is the only way to fight the devil. Scripture says:

OUT OF DARKNESS...INTO THE LIGHT

> *Thou wilt keep him in perfect peace, whose mind is stayed on thee: because he trusteth in thee.*
>
> *Isaiah 26:3*

Even though I was frightened, I persisted in reading my Bible and spending time with the Lord in prayer. This was my only defense against the enemy.

Many nights thereafter, I would awake with an oppression or force holding me down and I could not get up. In this state of consciousness, because of my awareness, I could actually see the spirit world and all the demons in it trying to oppress me while I was in my bed sleeping. They would whisper insidiously that Satan wants my soul and I had better not write this book. I would like to think it was just my mind playing tricks on me, but of course it was not.

One evening while I was writing, a friend called and asked if she could stay over for the night because she and her boyfriend were fighting. I said of course. When she arrived, I offered to let her sleep in my bed as I would be up late writing and would sleep in the den on the sofa.

In the early hours of the morning, my friend came running out of my bedroom screaming and crying, "Laurie, will you please come in here and sleep with me? I just had the most horrifying nightmare. I have never had anything like this happen to me before."

I asked her what had happened, but I already knew. She said she woke up and felt a strong force holding her down and she could not move. The bed was shaking and the potted tree next to the bed was shaking. I said, "Welcome to my apartment!" I lay down next to her with my Bible on my chest (as always). I prayed for God to keep us safe and allow us to sleep.

IN CLOSING

Trying to write this book has caused me many problems. The demonic spiritual attacks that I have encountered in the middle of the night are unthinkable. Poltergeist phenomena beyond what you could imagine. Many nights I have awoke only to find myself strapped down in my bed by moaning spirits. The only way I could equate this experience would be, imagine what it would feel like to wake up in a bed of snakes. I have endured many horrible things in order to put down on paper what I know to be the truth. The world needs to know what a terrible beast Satan really is. If my testimony can affect the life of just one person who may be traveling down the same road I once was, it is worth every sleepless night I have encountered!

In my efforts to share my true story with you, I have received help from many sources—from family members who have given me encouragement, from friends I have made in church who have prayed for my success in writing this book, and most of all from the Holy Spirit, Who has guided me all along and spoken to me through prayer and Scripture. My source of strength to fight this battle against the enemy is God's Word. Through God's Word I have discovered who I am in Christ and what power and authority I have in the name of Jesus. This is our only defense in spiritual warfare.

After reading many books on spiritual warfare, I found a church in Houston with a deliverance ministry. The process of expelling demons is called deliverance. Deliverance is not a cure-all. It is, however, an important part of what God is doing in relationship to the current revival in the church. My first step was honesty. Lack of honesty keeps areas of one's life in darkness. Demon spirits thrive on such darkness. Honesty helped to bring me into the light. Any sin not confessed or repented of gives a demon a "legal right" to remain.

Other steps I took were humility—recognizing that I was dependent upon God and His provisions for deliverance; repentance—by turning away from sin and Satan; renunciation—forsaking evil; and forgiveness—God freely forgives all who confess their sins and ask forgiveness through His Son, Jesus Christ. I also had to become willing to forgive others.

During my first session of deliverance when I forgave God for not changing my father, I actually felt a crack or release of my emotions which resulted in tears rolling down my cheeks.

Further steps I took through deliverance were getting rid of the "garbage" of years of damaged emotions that demons had attached themselves to.

I had to turn away from all my old ways of the past in order to have peace of mind and a peaceful life. I have to be very careful and live as clean a life as possible for, when sin "creeps" into my life, I become attacked by the enemy. Because of my "awareness" to the spirit world, I experience things others may never encounter when they sin. I have to watch closely every thought I think and I must be obedient to God. But the wonderful thing is that I am happier today and more at peace than I have ever been in my entire life. God is so wonderful!

Through this experience, God has taught me to glory in tribulations, knowing that tribulation produces perseverance, and perseverance produces character, and character produces hope. I greatly rejoice in all my trials which I've been allowed, to help keep me on the path of life. I am thankful and I give praise to the Lord, for He is my Redeemer.

God has completely changed my life and He has brought me to a place where I can now go forth and finish the work He has called me to do. I am so greatful to God for giving me back my life so that I may say to the world, **"I have sinned, and it did not profit me."**

> *He looketh upon men, and if any say, I have sinned, and perverted that which was right, and it profited me not; He will deliver his soul from going into the pit, and his life shall see the light. Lo, all these things worketh God oftentimes with man, To bring back his soul from the pit, to be enlightened with the light of the living.*
>
> *Job 33:27-30*

Not only has He given me a new life in Christ, but He has shown me that He is a God who does answer prayers. The many tearful years my mother spent on her hands and knees praying for my father and I. All of those prayers have been answered.

December 25, 1995

Dear Laurie:

> *I know in the past years, I was not the best Dad a daughter could have, but I have really tried to change. I have tried to make this Christmas very special for you. You and I have both changed. I am so very proud of you for your change, your book, your video tapes. Your change means more to me than if you had been a boy and made All American Football Player. Your change will lead so many people to Christ.*

> *I remember when you were just a little girl and I would put you in mom's little sports car and ride you around to show you off to all of my friends. I was so proud of you then. But now, I am even more proud of you!*
>
> *Laurie, You are a very special person! And I Love You With All My Heart!*
>
> *Thank God For You!!!*
>
> *Love, Dad*

Due to this experience I now have the Daddy I always dreamed of having. A Daddy who loves me! And a loving Father who has Blessed me!

Now I have become strong enough to talk about what happened and am able to share my experience with others. God has built me up through faith. He is the Rock I lean upon and it is His hands which lift me up when I am down. Thank you, my Lord!

Chapter Ten

LOOKING FORWARD

The New Age Movement is upon us and we are living in the last days. Every one is looking to spirituality for answers. Strangely enough, the New Age Movement is nothing but the old age mysticism, just wrapped up and packaged a little differently with advocates among groups from witches to humanists and scientists. Instead of turning to Christ and His church, people are filling their spiritual void with old-fashioned occultism dressed in the modern garb of parapsychology, holistic health, Eastern mysticism, and numerous cults marching under the banner of the New Age Movement.

The essence of New Age religion is that man is neither sinful nor evil and that the sacrifice Jesus made on the cross was meaningless and ineffective. Man does not need a Saviour to atone for his sin, say New Agers, because man has for many millennia been evolving toward perfection and godhood. New Agers suggest when we take a journey from within, we find that we are god; through channeling we can contact masters who have preceded us. This is a lie for they are communicating with demons from Satan.

> *This know also, that in the last days perilous times shall come. For men shall be lovers of their own selves, covetous, boasters, proud, blasphemers, disobedient to parents, unthankful, unholy, Without natural affection, trucebreakers, false accusers, incontinent, fierce, despisers of those that are good, Traitors, heady, highminded, lovers of pleasures more than lovers of God; Having a form of godliness, but denying the power thereof: from such turn away.*
>
> II Timothy 3:1-5

Attempting to meet spiritual needs apart from God is nothing new. The Bible tells us there will be massive apostasy during the last Church Age. The vast majority of people will fall prey to doctrines of demons. False prophets and false "Christs" will seduce people's minds and initiate them into the mystery of iniquity.

> *For the mystery of iniquity doth already work: only he who now letteth will let, until he be taken out of the way. And then shall that Wicked be revealed, whom the Lord shall consume with the spirit of his mouth, and shall destroy with the brightness of his coming: Even him, whose coming is after the working of Satan with all power and signs and lying wonders, And with all deceivableness of unrighteousness in them that perish; because they received not the love of the truth, that they might be saved. And for this cause God shall send them strong*

delusion, that they should believe a lie: That they all might be damned who believed not the truth, but had pleasure in unrighteousness.

II Thessalonians 2:7-12

We are soon to see one world religion and one world government. Satan is deceiving millions of people by having his demons pose as peaceful, loving, spiritual guides, guides to assist you and help you with your walk through life. These are all lies! Satan is a liar and a deceiver of men. Satan is taking over the minds of many through his lies and deceit.

This is the spirit of the antichrist working in the world today. To gain a greater foothold in individual lives, he develops programs to recruit people into spiritual slavery by their contacting spiritual guides and inviting demons in. In the end, he wants man to join him in his final battle with God. Meanwhile, like a con artist, he keeps as many promises as possible with the final price tag hidden.

The occult is rampant in America today. Due to the fact that man is increasingly apprehensive about the future. The Bible predicts an increase in satanic activity as we approach the end of age. After all, the time of the greatest recorded demon activity in all the history of time was just prior to and during the coming of Christ to the earth almost 2000 years ago. Does it not follow that Satan, the master deceiver of men, will increase his activities once again just before the Second Coming of Christ?

Satan has as many ways to deceive in the United States as there are interests among Americans. Whatever appeals to human beings can become a lure to the ultimate goal of self-worship and spiritual bondage.

Satan can use religion, health fads, pseudoscience, and a host of other covers to plant seeds that will eventually bear bitter fruit. Since there are an endless number of ways to be deceived, you can enter the occult stream at any point and eventually arrive at the same destination as your friends who stepped in at a different point along the way.

What requirement is necessary for a technique or practice to lead to the darker side of the spirit world? Just one: It must in some way violate the First Commandment:

Thou shalt have no other gods before me.

Exodus 20:3

Any object that purports to give supernatural guidance violates this commandment for the Scriptures teach that we should look to the true God alone for direction in our lives. Ouija boards, horoscopes, fortune-telling, and dozens of other such practices violate this basic principle. These practices are a substitute for belief and faith in the living God.

To the great majority of Christians, this means we must not worship any pagan god like Mohammed, Buddha, Confucius, or any other gods. But the metaphysical or spiritual interpretation of this commandment does not mean only that.

Of course no Christian would worship a statue, a crucifix, a religious relic, or any of the pagan gods, but when we put pride, resentment, criticism, condemnation, or hatred first in our lives, when we constantly think and act upon these thoughts, we are placing these things before God. In this way we deliberately break the First Commandment and, in so doing, we have to suffer the punishment that goes with it. God never punishes us; when we do wrong, we punish ourselves because in holding wrong thoughts, in performing wrong deeds, we, of our own free will, disobey God's teachings.

Likewise, the man or woman who puts money, social position, or other forms of false security before God is breaking this first law every day.

The average Christian would not like to be accused of bearing false witness, but do not many of us repeat idle gossip without proving the accuracy of our statements? And how many people mar their happiness by coveting other people's possessions, their success in life, their health, or their positive attitude towards life instead of going directly to their own Father in simple faith for these riches of the kingdom which He is waiting to pour out upon them to fulfill every righteous desire of their hearts?

I cannot conceive of a single person who could truthfully say he never breaks any of the Ten Commandments. However, when we do break them, we break ourselves for God's laws are immutable. When we break God's laws and do not repent and confess our sins daily, we leave ourselves open for attack. The Spirit, seriously grieved by sin *(Ephesians 4:30)* and quenched by gross disobedience *(I Thessalonians 5:19)* can offer no barrier to the invasion of satanic forces.

Satan knows how far he and his minions can go, and they will take every inch if allowed, or permitted to stay. By not repenting of your sin, Satan can introduce his thoughts into your mind, tempting you to act independently of God, as if they were your own thoughts or even God's thoughts. This is why it is so important to read and know God's Word. Satan's aim is to infiltrate your thoughts with his thoughts and to promote his lies in the face of God's truth. He knows if he can control your thoughts, he can control your behavior.

If you don't conquer Satan's temptation of your mind, you will begin to mull his thoughts over, consider them as options, and eventually choose to act them out. Repeated acts form habits, and if you exercise a sinful habit long enough, a stronghold will be established in your mind. Once a stronghold is established, you have lost the ability to control your behavior in that area.

Satan's primary aim is to promote self-interest as the chief end of man. Satan uses temptation by suggesting to your mind ways to serve yourself instead of God. Make no mistake about it—sin opens the door to demonic influence and Satan, but confession and repenting of your sins opens your life to God and His protection.

> *Likewise, I say unto you there is joy in the presence of the angels of God over one sinner that repenteth.*
>
> *Luke 15:10*

It is well worth taking the time to discover ourselves, to find out how, in a thousand little ways, we have broken God's laws. Let us then root out these evil characteristics, do something about overcoming them, and in so doing learn how to let God's laws work for us.

I have tried to present this story in such a way to reveal the truth of God's Word. Yes, we do serve a loving and faithful God. A God who offers salvation through His son, Jesus Christ. This salvation is freely offered to all who are willing to humble themselves and come before Him with a repentant heart. And by faith, accepting His grace and forgiveness.

But, He is also a just God, and His judgments are perfect. His justice is supreme. We can no longer continue to accept only, His love for us, without His law. For the love of God, without His supreme law is paganism... the doctrine of devils.

The true love of God includes the judgment of God. We must know both His kindness and His severity or we will forever walk in darkness. If we do not embrace both, we will always be in danger of deception and a fall from His grace.

While I realize there are those who are ever willing to know of His love, but very few to embrace His severity and justice. For those who will embrace this hard truth now, they will not suffer eternal loss. It is wisdom to know the love of God and the severity of God. It is wisdom to love Him and to fear Him!

The purpose of sharing my experience has been to bring you, my reader, **Out of Darkness...Into the Light!**

My prayer for you is that, if you do not already know Jesus Christ as your Lord and Saviour, you come to know Him in all His righteousness and fullness.

By faith, we are saved and only by faith will we be able to endure until the very end. Do not ever give up your faith in Christ Jesus our Lord, because God never gives up on any of us. His hand is always stretched out. It does not matter who you are or what you have done. His hand is *always, always still stretched out!*

Therefore is the anger of the Lord kindled against his people, and he hath stretched forth His hand against them, and hath smitten them: and the hills did tremble, and their carcases were torn in the midst of the streets. For all this His anger is not turned away, **but His hand is stretched out still.**

Isaiah 5:25 (emphasis mine)

Keep the faith, my friend, and may God richly bless you!

ABOUT THE AUTHOR

Laurie Wallace, author, has thoroughly researched Bible prophecy, the New Age Movement, and the occult challenge to Christianity. Laurie is a firm believer in the inerrancy of the Bible and salvation through Jesus Christ.

Laurie is currently the manager of a medical company. In her spare time, she hosts her own talk show in Houston, **"Keep Standing For The Truth."** She is a member of ProAmerica, Daughters of Liberty, and Texas Eagle Forum.

Laurie's present concern is for our children of tomorrow. With the United Nations Convention on the Rights of the Child, the UN treaty destroys the authority of American parents and violates the sanctity of our families. The doctrines of Eastern occultism are infiltrating our school systems by having students tap into a universal mind through meditation and contacting spirit guides.

Laurie's mistake of innocent dabbling with the occult is being taught in our school systems of today. Her focus is parents should be aware that to take children to school might mean that they are placed in the hands of the enemy.

Her vision is for Christian parents to stand against

the intrusion of Eastern religion into the classrooms of America. If not, we become an ally with Satan in his plans to rule the world and to take over the minds of our innocent children of today, and tomorrow.

> For Speaking Engagements:
> Laurie Wallace
> 2260 W. Holcombe Boulevard
> Suite 246
> Houston, TX 77030
> (713) 664-7249

FOR ADDITIONAL COPIES

For additional copies of **Out of Darkness...*Into the Light*,** please contact:

>Ambassador House
>P. O. Box 1153
>Westminster, Colorado 80030
>(303) 469-4056

Please send $14.00 (sales tax has been included), plus minimum postage of $2.00 for one book, and an additional .50 for each additional copy. Prices are subject to change.

The Last Word

By drawing on the power of Satan's demons to get what she wanted, Laurie had given them an incredible amount of power over her, so it was literally a life-and-death struggle from that point on to work with God to extricate herself from their clutches. But she and God won.

Laurie's story has a happy ending. It points, however, to a very sad situation. The enemy who entrapped Laurie is still on the loose!

Dr. Charles H. Kraft
Fuller Theological Seminary